CC
Comp.

COME to the FEAST

COME *to the* FEAST

*A Handbook for
Christian Women's Groups*

Lorraine A. Brown
and
Wilma C. Buckner

Dedication

To

D. and T. who let us BE
and
Frances A. who had her say

Acknowledgements

It is perhaps safe to say that none of this would have been written had we not functioned in leadership roles in the Women's Council of First Christian Church, Johnson City, Tennessee. Although the text, except where indicated otherwise, is of our creation, much of the material is based on our experiences with those wonderful First Ladies. We acknowledge our debt to all of them. Especially we want to thank Ottie Mearl Stuckenbruck, Rosalee Wolf, and Marileen Knisley for their outstanding examples of leadership and servanthood; Gail Phillips, Mary Ellen Lantzer, and Larry Van Dyke for allowing us to use their writings; Dorothy Roller for the superb work she has done with the newsletter, *First Ladies*; and Melanie Bowen for her contributions to the reading programs.

We also wish to acknowledge ideas gleaned from others in the Christian fellowships of which we have been members during the years.

It is our sincere desire that what has been written here will be used to the end that the Kingdom shall be advanced.

In Christ,

Lorraine and Willy
February 1, 1992

Table of Contents

The
Cutting Board

Preparing for Leadership

Chapter 1

Introduction

❖

What in the world are we doing writing a book for women to be used in the churches? After all it is 1990's. It's a question we had to ask ourselves as women who were very aware of the changes being sought by women in the service of their Lord. A young friend of ours recently illustrated this problem when she reluctantly agreed to serve as an officer in the women's council of our congregation. "I'm not even sure we need to have a women's group," she said. Coming from the NOW generation, she felt that women should be on the major committees of the church, serving as deacons - perhaps even elders - and so involved in the total life of the church that they would not have time for "women's work." Indeed, from her viewpoint, there would be no such thing as women's work for we would all be one in Christ, serving side by side to accomplish His work.

Our young friend has our sympathies. We understand the frustration of the young women - we have walked for years with bound hands and feet. We have known the days when women had to have women's work to be able to do anything at all in the church. We have lived through times when women's Bible study groups focused primarily on how to be good, submissive wives and mothers. We know of washing communion cups and baking communion bread, but being considered unworthy to pass the bread and wine. We remember longing for theological discussions, and not being satisfied with swapping baby stories and recipes with other women. We understand the dynamics of marrying a preacher rather than being allowed to be one.

So why are we writing a book in the 1990's to help women plan "women's work"? There are several reasons. The first is that women still need other women and always will. We have much to offer to each other. Through the years we have found that other women have most often been our role models, our spiritual shepherds who have called us to study, to devotion, and to growth in Christ. Women have been sustained by the care of other women in times of depression, illness, financial crisis, and spiritual dryness. We want to encourage women to continue these ministries to each other.

Secondly, like it or not, the church has not yet come to the stage of accepting women's gifts in leadership roles. If those gifts, such as leadership, administration, and teaching adults, are not to be buried, there needs to be an outlet for those gifts. Women's groups are for many women in many locations the only way within the church those skills and gifts can be used to God's glory. Certainly many women have found places of service outside the organized church and will continue to do so. For others, though, the church is the center of their lives and it is God's people they long most to serve.

In addition there is a scarcity of material to help women do a good job of serving. Not all women who find themselves in leadership roles are creative. Others are busy and need to have material readily available to make their tasks easier. Some are novices and need help getting started. Others are burned out, used up, and need the refreshment of new ideas, or old ideas restated. We hope to make this book meaningful to women of the 1990's by making it challenging, spiritually encouraging, and packed with ideas that can be adapted or used just as they are.

Finally, we perceive that this can be a book used by the whole church. Many of the programs are readily adaptable for Sunday School classes, fellowship committees, and other groups involving men as well as women. These can provide rich intergenerational experiences for the Christian community.

So on with the book.

Where Do We Begin?

—————❖—————

Whether your group is a fixture in the church, having been organized for the last one hundred years or is brand spanking new, the leaders of the group need to spend time in introspection before rushing into planning. The following questions need to be answered.

1. Who Are Your People? What are their needs? What are their interests? What are their ages? Where are they on the continuum of Christian faith? The group make-up has a great deal to do with the success or failure of your program. If you plan daytime activities for a group of people who work, you can expect poor attendance and a great many complaints. If you select milk of the word for your study when your women are rich in Biblical knowledge, you will miss a real opportunity to delve deep into the scripture.

2. What Is the Purpose of Your Group? Is this group to be primarily social? Do the people who attend come to study and have little time for refreshments and chatter? Do you have a specific focus such as missions, family life development, personal spiritual development, outreach to the community or greater church body? Is your group involved in a short term commitment or is it an ongoing activity of the church?

What do you wish to achieve? Most groups serve dual functions. People enjoy each other's company while working on a project, studying a series of lessons, or learning more ways to serve the missionaries. It is important, however, to clarify the primary and secondary purposes and communicate them to the whole group. If part of the people are looking for a good time and don't mind staying for hours just spending time with each other while the other half of the group is on a tight schedule and wants to get to the heart of the meeting which they perceive as Bible study, discouragement will occur and members are likely to drop out. In larger churches, it is possible to have a variety of groups functioning under one overall purpose but exhibiting wide diversity in their meetings.

3. How Does the Group Function Within the Overall Structure of the Church? Do you need the approval of the elders for all decisions made by the group or do you function independently, seeking the advice and support of the appointed leadership only as needed? Is there a mechanism in the church for coordinating your activities with other groups in the church? Groups in the church should not be put in any competitive situation where people have to choose between two or more activities designed for them. It is okay for the youth to meet at the same time as a women's group, but for the senior citizens to meet at the same time usually involves a conflict for many women. Take care to work with others in the congregation, and if the church is large you may want to work for a joint planning meeting of all group leaders in the church on a periodic basis to avoid overlapping of projects and events.

4. *What Kind of Leaders Are You?* Do you work well together? Do you try to do everything by yourselves and then become upset because you are overworked? Or do you include others in the work, encouraging them to develop their talents? Are you convinced of the need for good communication and do you practice openness of information? Do you work prayerfully and carefully, considering the needs of the entire group? Do you notice "silent people" of the church and try to include them in the group?

Once you have determined who your people are, who you are, what your purpose is and how you fit into the overall picture of the church you are ready to begin the work of planning and directing. May the Lord bless you as you work.

Note: Number one in the Appendix is a sample letter suitable for sending to your members at the beginning of the year. Feel free to use it as is or adapt it to your situation.

The Gift of Leadership

———❖———

The gift of leadership
Comes packaged in:
Fireballs who get things done in a flash
Before anyone knows what's happened;
Gentle spirits who inspire cooperation
From those who vowed not to get involved;
Organizers who know exactly what comes next
And give succinct directions to others;
Innovators who are full of surprises
And open up new ways of thinking and being.

The gift of leadership
Can be exciting,
Stimulating, frustrating, and lonely.
It can operate in difficult times
To the salvation of many
Or coast along in easy times, unnoticed.
But the gift of leadership
Can never exist alone.
It needs always as its companion
The gift of following.

For following and leading
Must go hand in hand,
With the leaders and followers
Sometimes switching roles

According to the demands of the road.
Because leading and following are both gifts,
The travelers need never fear
For their safety along the road.
It has been traveled before
By the Giver of All Gifts.

Wilma Buckner, 1982
Used by permission

The
Dough Bowl

Permeating the Year With a Theme

Chapter 2

Developing the Year's Program
Around a Theme

❖

While it is not necessary to follow a theme for the year, doing so provides continuity, makes planning of individual sections of the work easier, and encourages prompt attention to the outline of the year. Continuity is important because we have so little time at each meeting to make significant points. If, however, we use each facet of the work to build toward a specific emphasis, we are more likely to facilitate lasting change in the lives of the participants.

The selection of a theme provides direction for each program, avoiding the common question we ask, "What shall we do for our February council meeting?" Rather than floundering around in a world of possibilities, our question becomes, "What aspect of our theme do we want to emphasize at our February meeting?" By looking at the entire year at once, we can fit study material (for circle meetings), presentations for council meetings, service projects, budget needs, and social activities together into a coordinated whole.

Once you have decided to choose a theme, you can put to use the information you assembled in your introspective phase, Who are your people? What is the purpose of your group? And how does the group function within the overall structure of the church?

(See Where Do We Begin?) Three other things need to be considered at this stage of your planning.

The leaders must take into consideration the emphasis and/or study material of the last few years. If the theme of the last year has been intense and required much study, you might want to balance that year with a year of joy and simplicity. A year with a heavy focus on duty and works might be balanced with an emphasis on grace. A year in which social activities have been paramount may need to lead into a year rich in spiritual growth. Balanced studies over an extended period assure a well-rounded fellowship and meet the varied needs of a group.

Additionally, consideration needs to be given to the abilities of the leadership for the year. What gifts and talents do the leaders and the membership possess that can be used to the best advantage? One of the theme years to be presented in this section deals with a focus on reading. Leaders who were not serious readers would find such a theme difficult to present effectively. A focus on music in the life of the church might be appropriate if the leaders were musically inclined. This is not to say that all the leaders must be skilled in a particular area, but they should be conversant with the theme material so that they can be enthusiastic and able to select appropriate people to follow through on the theme.

One final item that needs examination is the kind of physical and financial demands a given theme would place upon the group. The choice of drama as a vehicle of Christian growth or expression may be a wonderful theme for a large church with access to props, costumes, talent, and a suitable place for presenting plays. A small church may want to develop a similar theme but may need to use role - playing, mime, and dramatic readings which would lend themselves to smaller areas and less outlay of money. Good stewardship of money and people power is essential for Christians.

We are presenting two complete theme years. They are yours to follow as given or preferably to adapt to your own setting. We hope you will be stimulated to develop themes that meet the specific needs of the saints in your congregation.

"Come to the Feast" and "Gather to Scatter" were themes used by Women's Council, First Christian Church, Johnson City, Tennessee from October 1986 through September 1988. The Women's Council was made up of all women of the church who wished to participate. The women were divided into ten circles (small groups) which met monthly for study, fellowship, and assignment of duties. The Council also held joint council meetings four times a year, in November, February, May, and August. The women, through their circles, provided the following services every year in addition to participating in the programs presented in the theme years: serving Wednesday night dinners, preparing communion, driving for Meals on Wheels, serving in a soup kitchen, laundering baptismal robes, and providing cookies for a children's home and birthday cakes for a retirement center.

Come to the Feast

———❖———

The theme for the year, "Come to the Feast," will focus on a reading program and emphasize our Lord's invitation to his feast. As a leader, encourage others to join you in participating in a feast of:

- Biblical study through the study of the book of Ephesians;
- words through the reading program;
- fellowship at "Taste and See," "High Tea with Mrs. Alexander Campbell," and "A Poke Party," three council meetings;
- memories at "A Taste of Childhood," an All-Daughters (Mother-Daughter) banquet.

Theme Verse: "Then he said to me, 'Son of man, eat what you find; eat this scroll, and go, speak to the house of Israel.' So I opened my mouth, and he fed me this scroll. And he said to me, 'Son of man, feed your stomach and fill your body with this scroll which I am giving you.' Then I ate it, and it was sweet as honey to my mouth" (Ezekiel 3:1-3).

The use of Ezekiel 3:1-3 as the theme verse is in keeping with the reading program. As members read (eat) books (scrolls), they can expect the sweetness of honey, but they also take on the responsibility of sharing the message with others. The theme verse can be printed on all material put out by the Council during the year. Members should be encouraged to memorize the verse and repeat it at circle meetings.

Theme Song: "All Things Are Ready" (come to the feast) can be used as a theme song if desired and sung at council meetings.

Biblical Study: With Christ in Heavenly Realms by Phillis Mitchell is recommended. This book, published by Aglow Publications, is a workbook study of the book of Ephesians. Any biblical study, however, would be appropriate for this theme year and we advise you to select something suitable to your situation.

COME TO THE FEAST READING PROGRAM

The Reading Program is the focus of this theme year. A well-designed reading program should include three things: the encouragement of Bible reading, the distribution of a reading list, and a reporting and reward system.

Encouragement of Bible Reading. In times past Bible reading was a common practice for Christians. Unfortunately in our busy world, many Christians rarely read their Bibles at home, and certainly not in any organized and consistent manner. The purpose of this phase of the reading program is NOT to make people feel guilty and condemned for not reading (a tactic often used in the past). The purpose is to encourage and to help people find joy and strength in reading. Many good systematic reading programs are available to help people develop the reading habit. The goal is to read the Bible completely in one year. Ephesians, or whatever book is studied by the group, should be read by every women, preferably several times in different versions of the Bible.

The Reading List is an exciting part of the program. The list should be assembled by a committee of avid readers. Notify them ahead of time that you would like them to attend a meeting and bring a list of recommended books. The books chosen should still be in print or available in the church or other local library. Devotional books, good novels, in-depth material, short articles and poems, prayers, and other books are appropriate. At the meeting, discuss the books recommended and divide them into categories (see below). If you have more recommended than can be used, have each woman rank her recommendations. You may also want to ask for recommendations from your minister, a seminary or Bible school professor or other respected reader.

The presentation of your reading list is important. If the list is presented like an ordinary bibliography, the chances are that very few will refer to it. Use colored paper, divide the books acording to type, and adopt a catchy format. The following menu layout is recommended.

Appetizers

Small portions of attractively presented devotionals, poetry, and prayers. A good starting place for the reluctant reader.

Examples: *Each New Day* by Corrie Ten Boom
Encourage Me by Chuck Swindoll
The Practice of the Presence of God by Brother Lawrence

Salad Bar
A variety of short essays, articles, devotionals, and stories on which one can nibble or make a meal.
Examples: *Touch of Wonder* by Arthur Gordon
The Home Has a Heart by Thyrea Bjorn
A Shepherd Looks at Psalm 23 by Phillip Keller

Spinach and Other Vegetables
Books designed to help you grow by strengthening your faith, commitment, and service.
Examples: *Freedom of Simplicity* by Richard J. Foster
Improving Your Serve by Chuck Swindoll
Prayer Time by Don DeWelt

Entrees
Meatier material, designed to be read as a unit, some short, some long, but all contain food for serious thought.
Examples: *Mere Christianity* by C.S. Lewis
Celebration of Discipline by Richard J. Foster
Meet Yourself in the Parables by Warren Wiersbe

Casseroles
A potpourri of pleasant reading, including biographies

and novels.

Examples: *Fool of God* by Louis Cochran
This Present Darkness by Frank Peretti
Green Leaf in Drought by Isobel Kuhn

Boxed Lunches

Materials suitable for reading out loud to shut-ins and family.

Examples: *The Best Christmas Pageant Ever* by Barbara Robinson
Dog Stories by James Herriot

Therapeutic Diets – Healing Meals

Books to help you deal with life's crises, pain, grief, death, disappointment, and family stages of growth. These are best read before the crisis occurs, but you may find them helpful during your pain.

Examples: *Good Grief* by Granger Westburg
You Can Get Bitter or Better by James W. Moore
When Your Friend Gets Cancer by Amy Harwell

Meals on Wheels

Books available on cassette tape for the vision-impaired, the busy, and others who prefer listening to reading.

Examples: *Improving Your Serve* by Chuck Swindoll

Bedtime Snacks

Little nuggets of devotional thought, prayer and beauty to end your day.

Examples: *The Singer, The Song,* and *The Finale* by Calvin Miller.

Mother's Milk

Read-a-louds for the very young child.

Examples: The Happy Day Books published by Standard Publishing

Frances Hook's Picture Book

After School Munchies

Books for children which teach Christian principles and Bible stories.

Examples: *I Found a Wishful Unicorn* by Ann Ashford

If Jesus Came to My House by Joan Gale Thomas

The Dangerous Journey a reprint of John Bunyan's *Pilgrim's Progress*

Pizza Parlor Specials

Fast, but nourishing food for the growing minds of teenagers.

Examples: *Nobody Else Will Listen* by Marjorie Holmes

You Gotta Keep Dancin' by Tim Hansel

As you can see, this is a rather lengthy list. You may decide to use fewer headings. Category length will vary with the number of books recommended by your people, with as few as three or as many as fifteen books being included in a category.

31

Reading Program Reporting and Reward System: This is the third essential ingredient of the well-designed reading program. It is vital that you realize that, important as it is, many women did not become "hooked on books" as young people. Some may have reading problems and have an antipathy toward reading. And in every congregation there will be some with impaired eyesight. Do not make these citizens who do not wish to report feel second class. This program should only be a whetting of the appetite. On the other hand do not forget those shut-ins who are readers. Having them send in their reports may be one way of helping them feel a part of the body. You may also want to count books read by mothers and grandmothers to children. Books recorded on tapes may also be counted if you choose.

You should, then, devise a reporting system that reflects your situation. Keep it as simple as you can so that your "bookkeeper" will not be too burdened. If you have a member who is "gung-ho" on reading, she may appreciate doing this. In fact, many such persons may lurk in your pews, but never attend a circle meeting. Such an emphasis may reach them. Appoint one person per circle as librarian. She may want to take a book box or basket with her to each meeting to make selection easier or more available. Members may want to lend their own books or buy a book for the traveling library. The librarian will also carry reporting slips for those wishing to report. It is suggested that these slips be filled out at home so as not to take time from the meeting proper. These slips should be turned in regularly to the reading program bookkeeper. The bookkeeping must be done conscientiously for the poke party or celebration feast at the end of the year to be rewarding.

Offering this reading program may be quite an ambitious venture, but we promise you it will taste like Ezekiel's honey to your lips. Many of our group thought it was the best thing we had done in the history of our council.

A sample report slip could include:

NAME _____ CIRCLE NO._____

Check if you have read EPHESIANS _____.
List any other Bible books you have read.

_____

_____

List any other worthwhile books you have read. Yes, novels may be included.

_____

_____

List any Christian periodical if you have read at least three articles.

_____

_____

On the back of this sheet list any tapes or books read to children or indicate whether you have finished the reading of the total Bible.

TASTE AND SEE
A "Come to the Feast" Council Meeting

Presented at the first of the council year, the "Taste and See" program serves to introduce the theme and the reading program.

Program Preparation: Your speaker for this meeting should be sold on reading. An *interesting* librarian can be used to introduce some good books or a storyteller can be used to tell stories from selected books. A delightful presentation can be developed using two characters who talk about the reading program with one being the comic and the other the straight person. Use puppets, people, or a mixture. Remember to contact your speaker or your players well in advance of the program. Keep the fun/interesting part of the program to fifteen or twenty minutes so the details of the reading program can be presented to the group by the Reading Chairperson.

If at all possible, the reading list should be ready for presentation at this meeting. It can be used in lieu of favors at the tables. The reporting forms should also be available at this meeting. Be ready to answer any questions people might have about the reading list or the reporting system.

Room Preparation: Decorations for the tables are simple. Books of various sizes and ages can be used, either stacked and tied with ribbons or opened to an interesting picture or reading. Ribbons can be stretched down the length of the table for added interest. If the meeting is in the autumn, bright leaves can be scattered around the books.

An attractive display of books from the church library should be placed to one side of the room for browsing before and after the meeting. They should be available for checking out. If the church has no library, now is a good time for planning one as a project for the following year. If it would work in your situation, you might ask a local religious book store to set up a display. The books could either be available for sale at the meeting or be purchased later at the store.

Suggested Program

Opening Song: "All Things Are Ready, Come to the Feast."

Prayer of Praise and Blessing: Thank God not only for the food if this is a dinner meeting or luncheon, but for the written word, the scroll which is like honey.

Council Business Meeting, if needed.

Music: You may want to have a solo or group. It would be fun and fitting for the entire group to sing The B-I-B-L-E. Suggested songs: "Wonderful Words of Life," "Break Thou the Bread of Life."

Scripture: Be sure to read the theme verse. You may also want to read the story of the Israelites listening for hours to the reading of scripture, II Chronicles 34:14-18, 29-33. Job's words in Job 19:23 are appropriate.

Taste and See: Presented by a speaker or as a dialogue.

Additional music: if desired. "Dwelling in Beulah

35

Land." (Speaks of feasting.)

Introduction of Reading Program: by the Reading Chairperson.

Benediction: (In unison) "Let the words of our mouths and the meditation of our hearts be acceptable in Thy sight, O Lord, our Rock and our Redeemer."

HIGH TEA WITH MRS. ALEXANDER CAMPBELL
A "Come to the Feast" Council Meeting

Introduction: High tea is usually held a little later in the afternoon than normal teas and the meal is more elaborate. Because attendance had not always been what we would have liked it to have been at our council meetings, we decided to hold one on a Sunday afternoon. In keeping with the theme, "Come to the Feast," a high tea seemed ideal. We also wanted to remember that the Feast we were inviting people to for the year was the feast of reading so we decided a book report would be in order. A normal book report seemed to be less than exciting so we settled on a dramatized book report. Our high tea became quite an affair but attendance was doubled and people still remember that wonderful occasion.

Timing: The time should be scheduled as late on Sunday afternoon as possible – allow about one hour for clean up before evening service and then back the starting time up two hours. Example: Tea 3-5, clean-up 5-6, evening service at 6. Choose a Sunday that does not conflict with other major church programs.

Program Preparation: Your book reviewer-actor may be a member of your congregation or an outsider. For our program we used the book, *Fool of God,* the life of Alexander Campbell, as the book to be reviewed. The story was to be told from the viewpoint of his second wife, Selina. Once this decision was made, our speaker was always referred to as Mrs. Alexander Campbell. Part of the suspense was that we never gave away her true identity until after the program. The reviewer should BECOME the person whose viewpoint is used, dressing in the clothes of the character's time with a small setting created for the delivery of the review. The key to success of such a delivery is to remember and behave as if the women were indeed in the home of the speaker, naturally sharing the life of Alexander Campbell as if with a friend.

Invitations: This is one occasion where individual invitations are recommended. They need not be engraved! but they should be small (regular typing paper folded twice) and unique. If someone in your group can do calligraphy, enlist her aid. The invitation should read, "Mrs. Alexander Campbell invites you to High Tea." Inside the invitation would give the place (Mrs. Campbell's Parlor – First Christian Church) time, and date. Invitations can be made on a regular copier. Of course, announcements should be included as usual in the church paper, and they should take the form of the individual invitations.

Room Decoration: Rather than use the large serving tables that most churches have, use card tables so that the room will have a cosy, parlor-like feeling. Borrow nice tablecloths, preferably white, from your members. Use lanterns and or candles for lighting on each table. Use old books, reading glasses, small potted plants and/or other small items on the tables for atmosphere. A long serving table can be placed to one side of the room on which the food is served buffet style.

Place the "stage" at a place where most people can see. Elevate it if possible. The scene can be quite simple. If *Fool of God* is the book you choose to review, the setting should include a table with an old lamp, teapot and cup, Selina Campbell in an old rocking chair – made up to appear very elderly and dressed like the mid-1800's. At her feet could be a bound packet of "letters" and perhaps some copies of books written by A. Campbell. A dog-eared sheaf of papers could be her copy of the "Declaration and Address." If you have a copy of a picture of A. Campbell, Bethany College or any old painting, it could be hung as a back drop.

Food: The food should be as elaborate as you can afford. You can stick with finger foods but should have both sweets and non-sweets such as vegetables and meats/cheeses. Both coffee and tea should be served. The teenage girls in the church can be recruited to refill coffee and tea cups after the ladies are first served from the buffet line. Make this a really super feast.

The Tea: After most of the guests have arrived, inform them that Mrs. Campbell has been delayed and would like them to go ahead and enjoy the buffet. Have the teenagers circulate, refilling tea and coffee cups, helping latecomers find seating, and collecting

38

the dishes when all have finished.

Begin the program proper with thanksgiving for the food and fellowship, and conduct any necessary business. Then introduce Mrs. Campbell, who greets the guests briefly as she makes her way to her chair.

Close the program with a song and/or prayer.

A TASTE OF CHILDHOOD
An All Daughter Banquet

Following the theme of "Come to the Feast," A Taste of Childhood invites the women of the church to remember their childhood and allows the younger ones to enjoy their own childhood. By using a book or story in the program, it also re-enforces the reading emphasis.

Program Preparations: Children should be a vital part of the program. If you have teachers in your congregation who are accustomed to planning programs, enlist their help in preparing a short program using the children. Some children may be used to lead as the whole group sings children's songs. Other children can be used in a dramatic reading of a children's book. *If Jesus Came to My House* by Joan Gale Thomas makes a delightful book to have the children recite. An option may be to have a good adult reader read some favorite children's story. Since children are to be involved, early planning and practice is essential.

Room Decorations: Let your imagination run wild as you drift off into childhood. Of course Teddy Bears and other stuffed animals can take a prominent place in the decorations. Large tissue fold-out ice cream cone decorations hanging from the ceiling add greatly to the memories of childhood. Suckers and other favorite candies can be sprinkled around on the tables or used as favors. Toys, especially dolls, can be used as centerpieces. Balloons, crayons and coloring books might also find a place in your decorating plans. Just use lots of color. This is one time it would be hard to overdo.

Menu: What would a taste of childhood be without ice cream for dessert – maybe even popsicles! Mashed potatoes and corn are also usually favorites of children. Whatever the menu, it should be rather simple food which reflects the tastes of childhood.

The Printed Program. A program cut in the shape of something related to the story or book to be read, such as a house if you are using *If Jesus Came to My House,* is suggested. You might include in the program a list of old tastes and new tastes of childhood. (See Appendix for pattern and lists of tastes.)

Suggested Program:

Prayer of Thanksgiving
Welcome (and business if needed)   President
Children's Songs   All Daughters
"My Mother Bids Me Bind My Hair"   Solo
   (May have mother plaiting child's hair as song is sung.)
Book dramatized by children or story by adult
Benediction: "At that time the disciples came to Jesus and asked, 'Who is the greatest in the kingdom of heaven?' He called a little child and had him stand

40

among them, And he said: 'I tell you the truth, unless you change and become like little children, you will never enter the kingdom of heaven. Therefore, whoever humbles himself like this child is the greatest in the kingdom of heaven' " (Matt. 18:1-4 NIV)

"Jesus Loves the Little Children"   Sung by All

POKE PARTY – A CELEBRATION FEAST
A "Come to the Feast" Council Meeting

"What in the world is a poke?" It is a question you will be asked often. The word is used by country folks and some of us city folks but a lot of people just don't know what a poke is. Webster defines it as "a bag or sack." The Poke Party came about because one of the authors in the congregation where this program was presented had written a book in which a poke party was described. We changed its nature to meet our needs and got a big kick out of closing our year with a poke party. We think you will, too.

Party Preparation: Because this is a party, a celebration, it is not necessary to have a speaker. Often the last program of the year will include the installation of new officers and that should be as brief as possible so awards can be given and a wide variety of people honored. Arouse people's curiosity with plenty of publicity about the Poke Party.

Menu planning will need to be careful and early. The food to be served is picnic fare, but should be of excellent quality. This special meal will be served in a

41

poke to be placed at each place before the people arrive. The following menu is suggested: congealed fruit salad, prepared in individual plastic containers with lids, one half of a pimento cheese on rye sandwich, one small croissant or one-half large croissant filled with chicken salad, small bag of chips, a slice of cheese cake. Be sure to include in the poke two napkins, a plastic spoon and fork. Of course the menu can be altered but be sure the food is above average quality. Frosted grapes would be a nice substitute for the congealed salad, and carrot cake in place of the cheese cake.

It is possible to buy white pokes in lunch bag size or regular brown bags can be used. It's the poke that counts, not the color. As favors, include an inexpensive bookmark in each poke. Bible book stores have very reasonably priced packages of bookmarks printed with Bible verses.

The Awards: This party is to celebrate readers and writers. Check to see if anyone (man or woman) in your congregation has written a book or article which has been published. If you have a large number, you may want to limit your awards to book authors or to those who have published in the last five years. Assemble a list of the authors and their publications for printing in the program. To honor the authors at the party, you can present them with colorful pads of paper and ball point pens or pencils for writing their next book.

The following readers should be honored: anyone who has completed a reading of the entire Bible in the previous year, even if they started their reading before your reading program began; all those who completed Ephesians (or whatever book of the Bible you have studied); the person who has read the most books; all the people who have read at least twelve books of the Bible and six other books during the last year; and anyone else you care to honor. Bible readers should get the best awards. Beautiful cross stitched bookmarks can be made if one plans early so that these will be given as awards. Bookmarks can be purchased inexpensively or expensively. Small blank books can also be used as awards for keeping a reading journal or record. Used books of good quality which are no longer in print make treasured awards. Be sure to indicate that the books are used and are carefully chosen for their valuable thoughts. If you begin early in the year to think and plan for these awards and look for bargains, you can use a minimum of money and give some special gifts. If you wish to honor some special person in the congregation or to remember those who have died during the year, a book presented to the church library would be fitting. All gifts and awards given should be presented in pokes, using all sizes and colors.

The Program

Provide picnic-type dinner music as people gather.
Blessing of the Food
Emptying of Pokes – the meal
Business Meeting, if needed.
Devotional – This should be planned around the importance of the Bible in our lives and the enrich-

ment we receive from reading books written by great Christians of the past and present. Scriptures can be used which have had special meaning for the devotional leader's life.

Musical Presentation, if desired.

Installation of Officers, if appropriate.

The Celebration: Reading awards, recognition of authors, and any special memorials.

Benediction: May the God of wisdom and insight bless you with wonder and a thirst for knowledge and understanding. May He grant that the words you choose to read be filled with truth and enrich you, and may you always walk with your hand in His, now and forever, Amen.

Gather to Scatter

A YEAR OF FOCUS ON THE BOOK OF ACTS

The theme "Gather to Scatter" is an outgrowth of a fresh look taken at the book of Acts. Though many good studies have been done on conversions, missionary journeys and other doctrinal issues, this study of Acts attempts to translate the activities of the early church into the reality of today. Included in the plan for this year will be:

- an outline for a ten-month study
- suggestions for combined circle meetings
- three council programs
- one mother-daughter banquet
- and guidelines for a reading list

The church first "gathered" on the day of Pentecost. That exciting and prophecy-fulfilling experience of the outpouring of the Holy Spirit was just the stage setting for the "scattering." Natural dispersion, persecution, and commissioning spread the Word and the works of the church. The "Gather to Scatter" theme and lesson material will follow the teaching and activities of those first century Christians and then call us to similar action in our time and place. Throughout the year you will *gather* to study and encourage one

45

another so that you may *scatter* to serve.

The *theme verses* come from Ephesians 4:11-13, which is a capsule statement of the purpose of our "Gather to Scatter" theme.

And He gave some as apostles, and some as prophets, and some as evangelists and some as pastors and teachers, for the equipping of the saints for the work of service, to the building up of the body of Christ, until we all attain to the unity of the faith, and of the knowledge of the Son of God, to a mature man, to the measure of the stature which belongs to the fullness of Christ (NASB).

Service will be the watchword for the year. Each woman will be challenged to identify her gifts and to find her place of service in the church and the community.

A *reading list* is suggested but not necessary. The list for this year, if used, should include reference works, studies in women's ministry, service-related material, and other interesting books. Bible reading and serious study of scripture should be highlighted.

THE GATHER TO SCATTER BIBLICAL STUDY

Purpose of study:

1. To become more familiar with the beginning and behaviors of the early church as reported in the book of Acts.

2. To become more familiar with the agencies and organizations available to people in need so that members can become resource people in many areas.

3. To encourage the use of gifts and talents individually and collectively in the service of others in the name of Jesus Christ.

Summary of the overall program:

1. The study of Acts. All women are encouraged to read the book of Acts at least once during the year. Six lessons from Acts will be presented.

2. The encouragement to serve. Four lessons will be presented in which the students will receive an overview of agencies, programs, organizations, and ways within the church and community through which Christians can serve those in need.

3. The extension of learning. Council programs will serve as a means of extending the individual's learning in the above areas, beginning with the meeting involving the discovery or affirmation of gifts.

4. The experience of field trips. While this is optional, interested persons in the group are encouraged to visit and get a firsthand glimpse of places where they may want to serve.

5. The personalization of reading. The women are encouraged to do special reading to expand their gifts. For example, a person possessing the gift of compassion might choose to read extensively in the area of ministering to the dying.

A Word of Explanation

Included in the outline are six study lessons from Acts – our gathering. Interspersed among the lessons on Acts are four lessons on service – our scattering.

47

These special lessons may be taught by the teacher but it is strongly suggested that guest speakers be used for these, either members of the congregation or community people who have served or are now serving in the areas under study. Suggestions will be made in the outline concerning these speakers.

There are several ways of approaching the scripture lesson. The teachers may simply study the scriptures given and develop their own lessons around the lesson topic listed. If time permits the teachers might want to get together before their circle meetings and discuss the scriptures and come to a united plan of approach. If you have a person gifted in writing, she could create written lessons which could be used by all teachers and distributed to all the women. Questions for each of the lessons in Acts are provided in the outline along with thought-provoking material to be used with the service lessons.

Lesson One
The Coming Together: The gospel
generates a fellowship in Jerusalem

Text: Acts 1:1-2:42

This lesson is crucial, for it sets the stage for the rest of the study. Try to look at these two chapters in a new light. Notice the verses you have not noticed before. Go back and study the Joel references. Hear the real message chapter two has for women. Be still and let the reality of the Holy Spirit fill you.

48

Questions

1. Why had the disciples "come together" in Jerusalem? (1:4,5). How was Jesus' purpose for the gathering different from theirs? What questions did they ask and what was his answer?

2. Why were they to wait? Do you think their questions (v. 6) showed them ready to begin their work? Why or why not?

3. What was the immersion they were to expect (v. 5)? How did they occupy their "waiting" time (1:14)? What practical matter did they take care of, and what O. T. scripture was the basis for their action? (Psalms 69: 25 and 109:8).

4. Upon whom did Joel say the Holy Spirit would be poured out? What were the people to do as a result?

5. What are some of the reasons members of the church today "come together"? Should our reasons be the same as theirs? How often does the Holy Spirit guide our actions? Does "waiting" play any part? If so, how do you think this time should be used?

Lesson Two
The Scattering: Spread of the Gospel

Text: Acts 8:1-8, 25-40; 10:1-48; 11:19-26; 13:1-4, 14-16; 14:26-28; 16:11-15; 18:12-17, 24-28; 19:1-10

Focus on what these scriptures say about the spread of the church. Try to learn facts for the time being. Who went where? Why did they go? Where did they

49

preach? What happened then? A careful reading aloud of these scriptures will have a real impact on your group meeting.

Questions

1. When problems arose in the church, what did the Apostles do to keep from being distracted from preaching the Word (6:1-7)?

2. What elements were involved in the appointment of Barnabas and Saul (Paul) as missionaries (13:1-5)?

3. Discuss what the following women did to help spread the gospel. Lydia (16:14-15, 40); Priscilla (18:1-3; 24-28, Rom. 16:3-5); Phoebe (Rom. 16:1-2); Phillip's daughters (8:9).

4. To what different types of people did Paul preach? Can you name others besides those listed (16:13; 17:16-34; 24:10; 26:1, 28)?

Lesson Three
Spreading the Word Today

Each circle (study group) should have a special speaker to discuss some phase of personal evangelism, world or local missions. Distribute a list of missionaries supported by your congregation along with addresses and brochures about missionary societies and church planting organizations in your fellowship.

Some Challenges of Evangelizing Around the World by Larry Van Dyke

A sensitivity-raising statement

There was a time in history when the barriers between the earth's people seemed to be mainly physical but today, thanks to jumbo jets, giant ocean vessels, towering antennas, microwave stations, and satellites, those earlier problems have been largely resolved. This does not end the matter, however. The barriers of culture, language and context still remain as great as ever. Let us consider these challenges to missionaries abroad.

The challenge is to think differently, but this is difficult. In Africa two men walk down the road holding hands. There is nothing unusual or perverted about this act of friendship, yet in our minds we cannot look at this behavior and not think it strange. We need to see with other eyes.

Few non-western societies have as highly a developed sense of technical time as we do in the west. Many facets of our culture, such as airline schedules and electronic communication, serve to make us extremely conscious of the need for split-second timing. The rural Filipino farmer may tell time by looking at the sun or the flower of the gourd. At five in the afternoon the edges of the flower have a certain bend. Learning to accept a different concept of time is a real challenge and begins with leaving the watch at home.

History to westerners has a beginning and an end. plus purposes to be achieved in the interim. History is

51

lineal and progressive. Time is on the march. But in other cultures, time is a very different sort of thing. History may be cyclical. It moves continually but in circles; and the circles themselves move very slowly. Life is bound to the wheel of existence. One existence follows upon another. Time is to be endured. The challenge is to communicate a purposeful God who is revealed in history.

When we hear the words "the dove and the fish" we picture two living creatures. In the language of Malawi, the expression "the dove and the fish" explains a complex and complicated story which brings meaning to the hearer. One may be able to speak the words but not communicate. That's the challenge of another language.

Middle eastern people are very impolite – pushy, loud, and rude – or so we think. Yet pushing and shoving in public is characteristic of middle Eastern culture and stems from a different set of assumptions. In the western world, the person is synonymous with an individual inside a skin. For the Arab, however, the person exists somewhere down inside the body. The ego is not completely hidden, however, because it can be reached very easily with an insult. On the other hand pushing and shoving is all right because it does not actually touch the inner you. The challenge is to understand this basic difference in body concepts.

Whether the servant of God goes to a far distant land or just around the corner to a radically different sub-culture, it is important to recognize the broad, all-inclusive nature of the gospel that transcends cultures and touches the very heart of humankind.

Lesson Four
Hurting and Healings: A world
in pain receives healing touches

Texts: Acts 3:1-10; 5:12-16; 8:4-8; 9:19-43; 14:8-10; 16:16-18; 18:1-12; 19:11-20; 20:7-12; 28:7-10

How easy it is to overlook the importance of these scriptures for they are, for the most part, very brief. Often the things we pay least attention to are the things that are very commonplace in our lives. As if it were as much a part of the life of the church as breathing is a part of life itself, healing took place on a regular basis. Look for the physical pain, the emotional hurts, and see what the church did to help.

Questions

1. Read the above scriptures and after each discuss the following:

  a. Who was hurting?
  b. What was the hurting?
  c. Where did the healing take place?
  d. Whom did God use to do the healing?
  e. What were the results?

2. To what extent does God expect us to be involved in helping and healing? Someone has said that Christians should either be "stretcher cases" or "stretcher bearers." Do you agree? Name some concrete ways in which we may be stretcher bearers.

Lesson Five
Daring to Touch Wounds

Each circle may chose a special speaker on such topics as child or wife abuse, chronic or mental illness to learn how to serve people better. This lesson lends itself well to joint meetings. Our congregation (a large group) had a morning session with three speakers and an evening session with three different speakers. Presentations took place simultaneously and members chose which they would attend. The speakers were a man from a local program for abused children, a woman from the domestic violence shelter, a cancer patient, a mother of a retarded child and others.

For this lesson, prepare a list of area agencies which provide help for the hurting and opportunities for service. We cannot help everyone who is ill or hurting, but we can become resource people, referring people to helping agencies or people. It is important to remember that *below the surface of any congregation of any significant size, major problems lie hidden. Handle all topics with sensitivity and love.*

The Bittersweet Pain of Birth Defects
A sensitivity-raising statement

All mothers-to-be long for a healthy baby, a whole baby. One of the most devastating things that can happen to a new mother is to be told that her child is not perfect, physically or mentally.

The following is a fictitious letter written by Josh, one of the imperfect kids.

To my Mom,

We fooled them, didn't we? You and I, Mom. We did it – together. Tricked the death angel out of one imperfect kid.

The nurses didn't think I was worth the fight – thought it would be easier on you if I just slipped on out of this world before you got a chance to get attached to me. They didn't know that you and I got attached way back when – when only God knew I would be born a mess.

Or did you know then, too, that I'd need a whopping big supply of love to pull me through the problems I'd have facing me? You must have known for you were so quick to embrace that bundle of physical abnormalities you had thrust upon you at my birth.

You didn't have the foggiest notion what the doctors meant when they told you I needed surgery for esophageal atresia. But you understood right quick that I had a real problem when they explained that the tubes to my stomach and lungs were joined. You knew that food and air just do not mix. And when they said I had hydrocephalus, you simply said, "Do what you have to to fix him." That should have been enough, but I got an infection from hanging around the hospital for so long. My heart couldn't handle all that, and the doctors thought for sure they were going to lose me.

But we fooled them, didn't we? You and I, Mom. You were a lover and I was a fighter. How could such a combination lose?

There's talk at the hospital that I'll be retarded. Maybe so, but then, maybe not. But who cares? We're

55

a winning team and somehow or another, we'll come out on top.

Oh, by the way, thanks Mom.

Your unique son,
Josh

Lesson Six
The Poor and Hungry

Text: Acts 4:32-37; 6:1-7; 11:27-30; 20:33-35; Scriptures of your choice from O.T. or N.T. – Proverbs is rich in references to the poor.

The early Christians shared their goods. They didn't do it perfectly so some got lost in the distribution, famine set in and help was supplied – the lessons in these brief scriptures are almost frightening to those of us with plenty. They deserve a careful study with supplementary scriptures from other parts of the Bible.

Questions

1. What extreme measures did the new Christians take to avoid the problem of having poor among them?

2. What things do you think contributed to the unfair distribution of goods? How was the problem solved?

3. Compare the prophecy of Agabus to the dreams

of the Pharaoh which Joseph interpreted. Compare the preparations made by each group of people.

Lesson Seven
The Poor You Have with You Always

Each circle should have a speaker to discuss such topics as local soup kitchens, World Vision, Bread for the World, or the homeless. Encourage each other to volunteer time, money, and food to meet the needs of the poor in your community and the world. Time spent serving in a local soup kitchen can be enlightening and humbling. Talk to the Presbyterians in your community about their program of donating three cents a meal for the hungry.

What About the Soap?
A sensitivity-raising statement

"Anyone can buy soap." Those words were spoken by a good man, my high school Sunday school teacher. Many things I remember about the man, but the statement he made in reference to the poor haunts me still.

"Can you get me some soap?" Those, too, are words that I remember. They were spoken over and over by a friend of mine who was poor. She didn't have money for soap. Even though different ones of us bought her soap often, she still was unable to keep her family clean and sweet-smelling. The odds were against her — a dirt yard, no hot water, crowded conditions.

Our stereotyping of the poor often leads us to self-justification of our lack of concern for them. The poor are not all lazy people who trade their food stamps to buy booze. The poor are not always dirty, foul-mouthed people who are not fit to go to school with our children.

Some of the poor are caught in a shifting economy. They are people who at one time were, or would be if they had a chance, hard working and able to care adequately for their families. Others of the poor have marginal skills and maybe even marginal intelligence. They cannot work because they do not have the capacity to work. Others have been overwhelmed by illness. If the breadwinner is able to work, medical expenses of a family member may take all of the pay.

True some of the poor are trifling, wicked people who steal what they have and add to the world's pain by venting their wrath on the unsuspecting. But even they are children of the Creator.

On Maslow's hierarchy of needs the poor find their place at the bottom of the chart, concerned with survival — food, clothing and shelter. We cannot expect them to clean up and seek self-actualization until we help them fill their bellies and find warmth on a cold winter day, and do it on such a consistent basis that they have no worry for tomorrow's food and warmth. There are people addressing those basic needs. You can be a part of those who care enough to get involved.

Soup Kitchen

We came together, the three of us,
To share the joy of serving.
Awkward and unsure we were,
But caring and willing to work.

We grated carrots, washed big pots,
And passed out plates of simple food
To grime-soiled, young laborers,
And tender children brought
By loving, abuse-marked mothers.
Others came unkempt, even drunk.
They were quietly withdrawn, tentative,
And often embarrassed and ashamed,
But all came hungry and in need.

We were humbled by their vulnerability;
Uncomfortably secure in our own wealth.
Then one day the face across the table
Was one with whom I'd shared better times.
She called my name, and I called hers,
Then we embraced, and differences dissolved.
So it was that on that lovely autumn day,
What we had long suspected, half believed,
We knew of a certainty to be true:
We all are seekers, hungry, needing,
And one eternal Giver serves us all.

Wilma C. Buckner
Copyright 1987, used by permission

Lesson Eight
Storms, Shipwrecks and
Persecutions: Risktaking

Texts: Acts 4:1-22, 29-31; 5:17-42; 6:8-8:4; 12:1-19; 13:49-52; 14:1-7, 19-20; 16:19-40; 17:5-9; Chapters 21-28.

What kind of church would it have been in those early days without those frightening experiences of storms, shipwrecks, and persecutions? Look for the strengths in the Christian victims. Examine their responses to the hardships. Consider the place of God during these hard times.

Questions

1. Identify in the scriptures listed above:
   a. The risktakers
   b. The risk
   c. The enemy
   d. The outcome

2. What risks do you take as you serve God? Can you recall times in your life when someone could have said to you as Mordecai said to Esther, "Who knows whether you have come to the kingdom for such a time as this?"

3. What is it that causes men and women to risk everything? Read Hebrews 11, esp. vv. 32-40.

Lesson Nine
Today's Risktakers

Each circle may have a speaker on how to support today's risktakers and provide safe harbor for them. Examples of risktakers are those who work with AIDS patients, those who champion unpopular but needed causes, and those who speak out for reform in the church. Many women are risking themselves for the kingdom. A discussion rather than a speaker may be in line for this lesson, for many women have burdens to share and no one to talk to about them. One of the risky areas of the church presently is the role of women in the church. Women need to help each others deal with this issue no matter what side each chooses to stand on.

Comfort Zones
A sensitivity-raising statement

Comfort zones. That's where most of us Americans live. Often when I stretch out in my queen-sized bed at night, I think of those who are sleeping in tents, in boxes, or under the sky without mattresses or adequate cover. My bed of comfort is symbolic of all my life. Physically, psychologically, financially, and spiritually I take few risks. Most of you reading this can identify with my comfort zones because they are yours, too. The following questions are designed to move us from comfort to discomfort and perhaps even cause us to risk something for the sake of all.

Do I dare risk:
- leaving an unsolved problem entirely to God?
- losing myself in order that Christ be formed in me?
- giving God the credit for my achievements?

How willing am I to listen to another person's views with the possibility that she may be right and I wrong?
- Could I be wrong about sexual issues?
- Do I need change and growth in areas of family relationships?
- Would I be willing to see God in a new light?

Do I take the risk of fellowshipping with different types of people?
- Do I count any mentally impaired people among my friends?
- Do I ever choose the company of blacks, whites, Hispanics, rich, or poor?
- Are any of my friends non-Christians?

How willing am I to devote even a short period of my life to a mission?
- Would I serve in South America for three years to preach the word?
- Would I serve for a year in a shelter for abused women?
- Would I go for three weeks to build shelter or minister to health needs of people in need?

How often would I give up time or an activity dear to me in order to minister to another?
- Would I give up my Women's Club to be free to teach children about God?
- Would I leave my bed unmade in order to take a cancer patient for an early treatment?

62

- Would I give up golf, tennis, a luncheon or soap operas to sit at the bedside of the dying?

Am I willing to extend hospitality to those outside my "comfort zone"?

- Am I willing to have someone who doesn't "smell good" sleep in my guest bed?
- Am I willing to have the church's richest member come to my small, poorly furnished apartment for lunch?
- Would I take an unwed pregnant girl into my home until the baby is born?
- If I discovered a person I had planned to invite for dinner was homosexual, would I still issue the invitation?

Dare I take the risk of becoming more than I have ever been, doing more than I have ever done, and walking where I've never walked provided Jesus goes with me?

Risks need not be huge to be risks. Little risks taken in our daily lives may bring changes in health, wealth, reputation, time, and power. Jesus turned the other cheek, associated with the undesirables of the world, took unpopular views religiously, lived a life of poverty, and endured abuse because he had a purpose. If, like Him, we have a goal, risks will be a part of our daily lives – included in our comfort zones.

Lesson Ten
Living as the Church: The realities
and purpose of gathering

Texts: Acts 15: 1-41; 19:24-41; General overview.

Sometimes we forget as we talk of restoring the New Testament church that the early church was at times a very fractured body. This lesson calls attention to the conflict and the solution. Play close attention to the role of the congregation and the Holy Spirit in this section.

Questions

1. Pharisaism dies hard. Do we place on new Christians yokes that come from our own views rather than set them free with the simple gospel?

2. Do we stress the good news that Jesus accepts all sinners just as *we* are and in whatever condition we find ourselves?

3. Are we afraid to ask the Holy Spirit for an answer because he may lay upon us something not very convenient?

4. Do we always feel God needs our human help?

5. Do we agree with Arthur Rouner's statement that what people are looking for in the church today is "the Spirit that can touch the heart, the Spirit that can move the soul, the Spirit that can speak to them of life and truth"? The church had it once; can *we* recover it?

6. How do we personally face conflicts? Do we care enough to confront? Do we face up to small issues before they become large ones?

7. How far would we be ready to go if our livelihood were threatened? How willing are we to pay a price for the faith we profess?

Optional Lessons 11 and 12

If your group meets all year and needs extra lessons, almost any of the lessons would lend themselves to discussion covering two months. The magnitude of lesson four makes it especially suitable for expansion into two lessons. A general overview would serve well as a final lesson.

Field trips are optional but would be a great addition to this year's work. Two months of a twelve month schedule could be used to acquaint your membership with area agencies. Select a mental health facility, a center for the developmently delayed (retarded), a county home for the aging poor, a children's home, a domestic violence shelter. An out-of-town trip to some facility supported by your fellowship would be very nice for a spring, summer, or autumn day. Know the places in your community where Christians can let their light shine.

GIFTS DIFFERING
A "Gather to Scatter" Council Meeting

In keeping with the third statement in our purpose for the "Gather to Scatter" year, the first council meeting for the year focuses on gifts.

Program Preparation: Select a speaker well in advance of the meeting time. The speaker may choose to give a self-graded test to determine each woman's gifts. A different approach may be taken by having a talk on the recognition and development of gifts. ELizabeth O'Connor books, *Eighth Day of Creation* and *Cry Pain, Cry Hope* are both helpful in discussing gifts and commitment. Contact those who will pray, read Scripture, and participate in the program in other ways. Be sure to get publicity out early.

Room Preparation: Tables can be decorated with empty boxes attractively wrapped. If money is available, purchase tiny colored gift boxes, put a Hershey's kiss in each one and use for favors. Seasonal flowers are always a nice addition and can be placed in open gift boxes. Ask persons who are artistically gifted to assist with decorations.

The Program Proper

Dinner Music: Ask a member who is gifted in music to play the piano or other suitable instrument as the guests arrive.

Prayer of Blessing: Is there someone known for their devotion to prayer? Ask them to lead the group.

Business Meeting: If needed.

Scripture Reading: Use Romans 12:3-8, and/or I Corinthians 12:4-31

Special Music: Select someone, or a group, to present a suitable song related to gifts, service or commitment.

"Gifts Differing": Suggested topic for speaker

Benediction and Scattering of Light: Have candles at each place. Darken the room and have the president or other leader light one candle at each table from a large candle that has burned at the head table all evening. The women at each table will light each

66

other's candles until all are burning. Following the benediction, the women can leave the room with their candles in silence or as the pianist plays, "I Would Serve Jesus."

SCATTERING SEEDS OF LOVE IN A WORLD OF DARKNESS
A "Gather to Scatter" Council Meeting

Program Preparation: There is a warmth about music that gets any occasion off to a good start. Background piano music or quiet taped music is a good way to start this program on love. The songs can be songs of the church such as "Love Lifted Me," "O, Love, That Will Not Let Me Go" and "My Jesus, I Love Thee," or can be popular love songs of high quality. If this is to be a tea or dinner meeting, have the music continue through the meal.

This program should provide a *focus* on love, an *inspiration* to love and a *challenge* to love. The *focus* begins with the prelude and dinner music and comes to a high point with vocal music to introduce the body of the program. Solos or group music can be used. Nothing is more inspiring or more touching than stories. Several people can be used to tell stories of love from their own experiences or one person can tell a series of love stories.

The *challenge* should be based on the theme your group wants to pursue for the year. It can be an emphasis on love for the world, love for a community group, or love within the church body. Because loving one another can lead to loving others, it is recommended that each person pick out someone she doesn't know very well and love that person for the coming year. That love is to be demonstrated in personal contacts through visits and hospitality, prayers, and any other ways that seem appropriate. The expressions of love should be genuine and the person should not be told he/she was chosen as the result of a challenge. The group should be reminded frequently of their love commitment throughout the year.

Room Preparation: The red of love and the black of darkness should be the colors used for decoration. Red hearts (love) and black balloons (the world) can be used in a variety of ways. Black ribbons down the center of the tables with various sized paper hearts placed along the ribbon, or clay pots painted black with bouquets of hearts growing out of them are just two ways the theme could be carried out.

Program Presentation

Instrumental medley of love songs
Prayer of praise and thanksgiving to a Loving God
Welcome, business meeting
Reading of Love Scriptures
Vocal solo
Love Stories
Challenge to Love more fully
Benediction
Group singing of "We Are One in the Spirit"

A GATHERING OF LAUGHTER
An All Daughters Banquet
A "Gather to Scatter" Affair

Program Presentation: "A Gathering of Laughter" follows a circus theme. Planning and preparation are tremendous undertakings and should begin months in advance. The whole program centers on the performance of acts by children, both boys and girls. Many children take dance lessons, acrobatics, and other classes which make them well suited for performing circus acts. Other children can be clowns, wild animals, strong men, or take part in a band. Care should be taken to secure the children's safety. Tumbling mats should be provided for the acrobats; tightrope walkers should walk wide planks carefully secured just above the floor. Suggested acts are listed in the program proper but each group will have to assess its children and plan accordingly. As many adults as are willing should also dress in clown costumes. Costumes may be as elaborate as the budget allows but can be illusionary, using play clothes with masks or face paint. An interesting twist would be to have mother-daughter acts.

Publicity: This occasion deserves lot of hype! Use colorful posters everywhere they are permitted. (Posters can later be used to decorate the room.) Clowns and wild animals can be put on all advertising.

Room Preparation: For the circus, the tables should be set up in a circle with a large area for performance left in the center. A wide aisle should be left for the entrance of the performers. The more elaborate the decorations, the more like a circus it will seem. Balloons are a must. Bright colors, streamers, circus or animal posters on the walls, confetti sprinkled on the tables (if you are willing to clean it up), boxes of animal crackers (the ones like circus trains) all add to the atmosphere. Long, wide strips of cloth or streamers draped from a center point can give the illusion of being in a tent. Big stuffed animals borrowed from the children can be used around the room. Being both realistic and imaginative with your budget, you can create a real circus atmosphere.

The Menu: If your group is willing, you can have hots dogs, french fries, popcorn, and other circus food. If you have many older people, it will probably be necessary to choose a more conservative menu. The children might still be served hot dogs, bananas, small bags of popcorn or peanuts and big cookies.

The Program Proper

Opening Prayer
Introduction of Circus Acts by Ringmaster/Ringmistress
Acrobats
Tightrope Walkers
Junior Clowns
Animal Band
Clown Magician
Circus Cats
Strong Men
(Background music can be played during the silent acts.)
Brief Intermission
Grand Finale – Parade   Marching Music

Serious Thoughts on Laughter: This should be a very short devotional including some scripture such as Nehemiah 8:10-12, Psalms 5:11-12; 20:2; 33:20-22.

Benediction: May the Lord of Laughter fill you with giggles and cause happiness to rain upon you. May the joy of your strength always remain in the One who made heaven and earth. Go in pleasure and peace. Amen.

THE THRESHING FLOOR – A HARVEST OF DEEDS
A "Gather to Scatter" Council Meeting

Introduction: Everybody and every organization should do a personal evaluation occasionally. Year end is a good time for such an evaluation and "The Threshing Floor" is that time for the "Gather to Scatter" year. Evaluations call for new goals and sometimes for changes in direction and leadership so installation of new officers is a part of this program.

Program Preparation: The outgoing officers need to collect a list of accomplishments from each of the circles and compile a list of the Council accomplishments. This should include monetary gifts, services, visits, projects and so forth. It is also important to think of the things that were planned but never completed, goals set but not reached, mistakes made, and recommendations for improvements. This report can be prepared in written form or given orally by the officers. Preferably it should be given in written form and referred to briefly by the President at the meeting.

If one of your service projects is ministering to the

aged and shut-ins, prepare a list of their names and pay tribute to them and those who served them. Any members whom you wish to honor for their goods deeds during the year should be determined. A speaker should be selected to install new officers.

Room Preparation: If serving a meal, decorate the tables with wheat or other grains, and harvest fruits and vegetables.

Program Presentation

Opening Prayer	Voice 1
Welcome, Business Meeting	Outgoing
Evaluation Report	President
Celebration in Song "Bringing in the Sheaves"	All
Awards (Reading Program, Service, and so forth)	Voice 2
Honoring of Shut-ins and Their Servants	Voice 3

A Moment of Silence in honor of members and friends who have died in the past year. (Allow time for the naming of these by the group.)

Speaker Introduction	Voice 4
Installation of Officers (See below.)	Speaker
Response and Closing Prayer	Incoming President
Sing "Sowing in the Morning"	All

Suggested Installation Service

Installation Officer: For any harvest, there must of necessity be the planting and tending of the crop. The new officers you have elected will be the crop planters and tenders, but you, the followers, must assist them in the task by being good soil, nurturing the seeds of their leadership and making their tasks of tending the crop easier.

Will the leaders for the next year please come forward to accept our commissioning and our support?

_____, you have been elected President of this group of women for the coming year. It will be your task to take the seed ideas of your office and plant them in the lives of your friends and co-workers. You will want to plant the seeds of kindness, service, Bible study, prayer, and stewardship and to demonstrate the fruits of those seeds in your life. As a reminder, we would like to give you this package of seeds and commit ourselves to being rich and fertile soil.

_____, you have been elected to be Vice-President of these women. It will be your job to support the President and assist her in nurturing the tender plants. We would like you to have this watering can so that you, like Apollos, can water what your President has planted.

_____, you have been elected Secretary for the coming year. It is your job to make note of the plants' growth, reporting back to the other officers and to the members so that they can be aware of their

73

progress. We would like you to have this container of fertilizer that can be applied if your records indicate that the plants need growth.

_____, you have been selected as Treasurer, to count the harvest of funds that grow forth from this group. We would like you to have a basket to take in the fruits of this Council's labors.

To all of you, we trust you to encourage our growth in the work of the Lord, that we may bring forth fruit worthy of our Master.

The
Bread Basket

A Collection of Individual Programs

Chapter 3

Making Music Together
Sharing Memories
❖

A PROGRAM BUILT AROUND MUSIC BOXES

Program Preparation: Guests/members should be asked ahead of time to be prepared to share the memories associated with the acquisition of their boxes. Besides enjoying the stories themselves, you may want to award some prizes for the oldest box, the most unique, the most recent gift, and so forth.

Room Preparation: Preparation for this program is easy. Table decorations for a luncheon or dinner meeting consist of inviting the members/guests to bring their music boxes with them to the meeting to use as centerpieces. These along with some colorful napkins will be sufficient.

Program Presentation

Music: "In My Heart There Rings a Melody"
Scripture: Genesis 4:19-22. "Lamech married two wives — Adah and Zillah. To Adah was born a baby named Jabal. He became the first of the cattlemen and those living in tents. His brother's name was Jubal, the first musician — the inventor of the harp and flute. To Lamech's other wife, Zillah, was born Tubal-Cain. He

77

opened the first foundry forging instruments of bronze and iron." (Living Bible)

History of Music Boxes: God made the first music box when He first made man and woman. Perhaps they were the first to sing praise to God with their voices. Is it too much to imagine that the first love song was sung by Adam to his lovely Eve? Part of the beauty of Eden was surely in the melodic sounds the first man and woman enjoyed: the wind sighing in the trees, the tinkling of streams, the myriad songs of birds. The minds of these created beings were filled with the simple joys of life and music was among them.

After the fall and expulsion from Eden, it was not until the eighth generation that we read about the making of instruments. Were these people too bent under the load of wrestling a living from alien soil to be creative? At any rate it is interesting to trace the development of "automatic" music from primitive beginnings to the sophisticated instruments today — from the simple ones of Jubal to our modern organs and exquisite flutes.

The carillon was probably the earliest form of mechanical music as we know it today. The carillon were cymbals which were tuned to pitch. These were found in China where they were probably used for thousands of years. Early in the fourteenth century an English monk developed a bell-ringing device in a tower clock. This mechanism energized life-sized figures to strike bells on the hours. In Latin countries sacred music was played by these clocks on Sundays and folk songs during the week.

From these large tower clocks developed the concept that if large hammers could be made to strike huge bells to produce music, why could not watchmakers make tiny hammers to strike tiny bells? In 1601 two German watchmakers made an automatic musical clock to present to their emperor. In 1676 the repeater watch was invented and in 1730 the first Black Forrest cuckoo clock. It was the Swiss, however, who in the middle of the 18th century found that by turning a key, the clock's wound spring could unwind a melody even while keeping the time. It is this concept that gives us today's music box.

The music box was popular because it was small and thus could be moved from one place to another. It also was relatively inexpensive and available to the ordinary citizen. It was popular for about one hundred years until the invention of the Edison phonograph and the player piano, both mechanical music boxes themselves.

Perhaps you can remember the steam calliope played by circuses and the Mississippi River boats. The calliope was dangerous because the music was produced by steam escaping through pipes which often blew up, scalding the musician and often blistering the keyboard.

So, as can be seen, although we usually think of the small boxes which we have today, there are many instruments of music which can be called music boxes. Music boxes are back in favor today and are symbols of some of our happiest and most intimate moments.

Sharing Our Music Box Stories and Awarding of Prizes

Closing: Close "Making Music Together" by having all play music boxes together.

Benediction: May the Lord of rustling leaves and songbirds fill your heart with music and your lips with songs of praise.

Notes: In your community there may be many examples of mechanical music boxes (such as the older phonographs which used hard, grooved cylinders) available for sharing. If their owners do not belong to your congregation, this would provide your group the opportunity to invite them to join you.

This program is ideally suited for Senior Citizen groups, adult Bible classes or, with adaptation, All Daughters Banquets. This program would, of course, be a fitting one for civic groups, such as music clubs.

Ship Ahoy
A Father and Son Fellowship

❖

Room Decorations: Since this is to be a cruise, a gangplank should be arranged for and guests should present their boarding passes. These are tickets issued previously when reservations are made. A nautical theme may be carried out in red, white and blue flags, life jackets, life boats, and lounge chairs. Tables may have white cloths with alternate napkins in red and blue. (We suggest that planning this event for February or July would make decorating easier because of the availability of the red, white and blue items.)

Napkins may be folded in boat shapes if desired. Centerpieces may be toy boats, flags and/or balloons. Programs should be printed as cruise folders and candy Lifesavers used as favors. A captain's table will seat the persons to be on the program.

Program and Dinner: The captain, in uniform if possible, should welcome the guests and ask the ship's chaplain to ask the blessing on the food. Food may be served by the ladies or a buffet can be arranged in the "galley." Music can be provided by brass instrumentalists, or tapes of martial music would lend atmosphere.

At an appointed time in the program, pirates in costume will board the good ship *FAS* and arrest some of the guests for various misdemeanors (real or created for the occasion) and made to walk the gangplank.

They may also want to "rob" certain ones of their watches and money. The pirates disappear when another ship is sighted coming to the rescue.

Close the evening with a devotional by an elder on the importance of 1) Setting one's sails, 2) Staying on course, and 3) Arriving at the intended destination. This devotional should not be too long or too involved — keep the children's attention spans in mind!

Channels of Love
A Quilt Show
❖

Room Preparation: This theme is very easy to carry out in room decorations. Quilts may line the walls, be placed over quilt racks, stools, or even ladders. Tables for serving lunch or dinner may use gingham tablecloths with centerpieces of small sewing baskets with supplies, dried flowers, oil lamps or candles, and/or old books or photographs.

Program Preparation: Working well ahead of time, survey your membership to see how many have quilts to share. (Friends of the church may wish to display their keepsakes also.) Since they preserve precious memories, it is imperative that you make every effort to keep the quilts safe. For this reason, it would be advisable for quilts to be brought the same day of the display unless it is possible to secure them otherwise. Quilts should be labeled as to the owner, the name of the pattern, the name of the quilter(s), with any notes of interest the owner wishes to share.

Program Presentation

Music, a "patchwork" of hymns or "ol' timey" songs.
Poem, "Patchwork Days" (see below).
History of Quilting (See below).
Quilt Show (See below).
Tableau or skit (See below and appendix, #3).

Benediction: This prayer should express gratitude for our precious memories and for the lives of those who have meant so much to us.

PATCHWORK DAYS

Written in honor and memory of Mary Putman by Wilma C. Buckner.

Your hands are smooth and idle now,
But I am told of winter nights
When once you sat long after dark
And pieced together bits of cloth;
A bright red, square, a green, a gold,
'Til beauty sprung from your dear hands
In patchwork quilts to warm the night.

No more quilts will strength allow,
But you are piecing bits of life
Into a patchwork blend of people's lives.
Children, grandchildren, great ones, too,
All their lives are patterned by you.
And gently even now you bind —
One square a somber grey of pain,
The next a bright and laughing day.
A joy, a tear, a crock of kraut
Are bound together good and tight
With threads of tenderness and love.

These patchwork days that you are sharing
With strong young men and caring daughters,
A kind old man and little children,

And all the others you are touching
Will bring a warmth much longer lasting
Than a thousand fabric patchwork quilts.
Our life is made of stronger stuff
Than cotton, wool, and man-made fiber.
This time of learning, suffering, holding,
Will mark our lives and leave on us
A golden applique of loving.

Copyright 1984 Used by permission

History of Quilting

Quilting, as far as we know, originated in the Far East in the 11th century. It was brought west by returning Crusaders and soon erupted into banners to be carried into battle. These appeared as pieced work and also in elaborate appliqued designs.

By the time of the Middle Ages quilts were used in a variety of ways. Necessity being the mother of invention, it was natural that they be used mainly for warmth, such as bed drapes to keep out drafts and "the layered look" in women's clothing among the royalty who could afford it. Handwork became popular in the reign of Queen Elizabeth, who decorated much of her own clothing with intricate designs in pieced work, applique and embroidery.

The praise for the beauty and ingenuity of quilts in today's world in the U. S. belongs to that hardy and thrifty generation of early American women. With little resources, they often had to prepare their own materials and dye; and so not a scrap was wasted! Cutting bees as well as quilting bees were social outings for women who had no time to waste. Each woman would bring her pattern to share and each would exchange materials so each would have a variety.

It is being said today that with little leisure and almost no opportunity among the common woman for self-expression, quiltmaking has become her avenue to creativity. Marjorie Puckett, in her book on shadow quilting, states, "I have learned to see needlework as a very strong expression of many feelings, including pain, boredom, disappointment, loneliness, love, joy, and sometimes tremendous exuberance." Quilts have stories to tell!

Quilt Show

This presentation can be handled in great style or very simply. With a microphone and flood light one can highlight one quilt at a time with an emcee using the material handed in with each quilt to describe each quilt. If you prefer, however, time could be set aside for viewing before or after the general meeting.

Tableau or Skit

An effective skit can be written using three generations of family, demonstrating that quilts are indeed "channels of love." The skit could center on a family discussion around an old trunk and its contents or perhaps on a treasured quilt the grandmother has on her bed and wishes to pass on to her granddaughter. See sample skit in Appendix.

An alternate tableau can be given with the actors (the grandmother in bed covered with a quilt being attended by her daughter and granddaughter) forming a "still life" picture while a reader off to the side reads the poem "Patchwork Days." In this case, the poem would be omitted earlier in the program.

The Gift of Grandmothers
An All Daughters Banquet

What could be a better theme for a banquet than a celebration of the gift of Grandmothers? What is the legacy bequeathed by these special women in our lives? For each of us it is different. This program will bring to remembrance those enduring relationships.

For this program we are offering a number of alternatives because there are so many ways to develop this theme. We encourage you to select the program that meets your needs.

Recipe book: Well in advance of the banquet, have your women turn in recipes passed down to them from their grandmothers. Type these and create a recipe book, *From Granny's Kitchen,*which will be distributed at the banquet. For interest you might add a few Grandmother tales. A homey sketch of the vintage stove our grandmothers may have used would make a delightful cover.

Room Decorations: Items that were inherited from

grandmothers can be solicited and used as table decorations. If this is done, valuable items should not be brought until the day of the banquet. Every item should be labeled with the owner's name.

OR: Petunias in small tin cans, reminiscent of the large cans many grandmothers had on their porches years ago, can be used on the table along with drawings and definitions of grandmothers provided by the children of the church.

Fun Things To Do

1. Have people bring pictures of their grandmothers. Create a rogue's gallery on a wall or table, number the photographs and let people guess whose grandmother is who.

2. Of course there is always the recognization of the oldest and youngest grandmothers, the grandmother with the most grandchildren, great grandchildren, the youngest grandchild and so forth. Picture frames or albums and brag books would make neat prizes for those honored.

3. Before the banquet solicit from the grandmothers items of advice and colorful expressions from long ago. Read as many of them as possible at the banquet. You many want to use them in the cookbook.

4. Have all the grandchildren whose grandmothers came with them to the banquet put their names in a hat and draw one or two names. Present these children with a gift certificate to take their grandmother to McDonald's (or a finer restaurant if you so choose) for dinner.

5. See how many names for Grandmother can be identified by the group.

Planning the Entertainment

Have a granddaughter, daughter/mother, and grandmother talk about grandmothers. Each one should be brief for a TOTAL of no more than 10-15 minutes.

OR: Have a very informal program with the singing of songs grandmothers sang to their little ones. Then allow people in the audience to tell stories of their grandmothers as time allows. These are very entertaining and will evoke memories from the listeners also. Be sure to have a portable mike if you do this so everyone can hear.

OR: Have a skit which depicts grandmothers of the 1890's and 1990's. That early grandmother no doubt will be one with many children around her feet and a big pot of soup on the stove. The 1990's grandmom might be a professional woman who takes her one grandchild on a tour of her work place. The characteristics of love and warmth should show through in each woman. Or the skit might have grandmothers representing several generations sit around a table for a discussion of the changing role of grandparents. Interruptions by grandchildren dressed in vintage costumes would add to the interest.

As you plan, don't forget to have a devotional with Scripture and perhaps a sentence prayer of thanksgiving for grandmothers.

Oriental Holiday
An All Daughters Banquet
❖

The invitation to an All Daughters Banquet seems to the authors to be more more inclusive than one to a Mother/Daughter affair. While all women have not been mothers and others may never have had a caring mother, all have been daughters. The term All Daughters takes care of any awkwardness some women may feel about attending.

Room Preparation: The Orientals have many festivals through their calendar year, and their preparations are very elaborate. This theme can be fun to carry out in your decorations. Each table may be set exactly like the others, but with a wealth of collected items, each table can be different. The choice of napkins is very important, for they are able to unify the whole. Choose three different colors or shades and your room will come alive immediately. These napkins should be folded in an accordion fan shape and placed in the water glasses or secured in the middle with pipe stem cleaners long enough to be twisted into butterfly antennae.

For table decorations, you may find among your membership or friends such items as figurines, rice bowls, fans, teapots, tiny tea sets, china cups and saucers, silk flowers, small lacquered items, miniature kites or umbrellas. Larger items to be used around the room might be flowered fire screens, pictures or posters of oriental people or scenes.

Program Preparation: The program for this banquet may give you occasion to hear a missionary speaker or a national from the Orient. In this case you may want to provide a lighter touch by using the tangram puzzle at the table, especially but not exclusively for the children. (See Appendix #4)

You may, instead, want to invite a local florist to give a presentation on flower arranging, including at least one oriental piece. You may want to award a single blossom to the oldest daughter, the youngest, and the daughter who has the largest number of family members with her. There may also be a prize for the daughter who traveled the most miles to attend. You may wish to award a flower arrangement done by the florist to some special person.

Food: You should remember that many daughters may be children. Thus American food, including rice, is suggested for the meal proper. In a separate welcoming area almond tea and fortune cookies may be served before the meal. (See Appendix #5 for tea recipe.)

Program Presentation

Tea and Cookies
Invitation to be seated for dinner
Blessing for food
Dinner with background music
Welcome and introduction to program (If you are using the puzzle, use it before the speaker.)

Program (your choice)
Awards
Benediction

Note: It is possible you may have a vocalist that can sing some music from Puccini's *Madam Butterfly* or other such selection. If such is not the case, dinner music may be provided by piano, flute, or violin. Atmosphere may also be provided by hostesses and/or guests wearing kimonos.

New Wineskins

❖

Installation Services

Chapter 4

Celebration of Servanthood
An Installation Service
————❖————

It is important that the church as a whole be informed as to the service the women are rendering. It is always a bit dismaying to find that all too often those not involved are uninformed and perhaps as a result seemingly unappreciative of the tasks performed instead of being encouraging and helpful. For this reason it is good to have the installation of officers held at a regular service if at all possible (a Sunday night service is recommended). It is also important that the officers being commissioned be impressed with the charge which they are accepting, and such a special service helps to emphasize that.

Program Preparation: Each officer will be presented with the emblem of their service, a towel imprinted with the scripture reference, John 13:14, "If I then, your Lord and Teacher, have washed your feet, you also ought to wash one another's feet." If white, institutional grade hand towels are purchased, the cost can be kept to a minimum. These or any others having a plain white band across the end can be used. "John 13:14" can be printed on with liquid embroidery found at craft stores or departments.

A number of women representing all ages should be used in the worship program. These should be asked well in advance.

Room Arrangement: Since the emblems for this service of Servanthood are the basin and towels, arrange a table with an old fashioned bowl and pitcher and the towels which will be presented in the service. If you are in the sanctuary, it might be possible for this table and the one used for communion to enhance each other since the symbols for both were introduced at the Last Supper.

A Celebration of Servanthood

"As each one has received a special gift, employ it serving one another, as good stewards of the manifold grace of God." I Peter 4:10

Call to Worship   Voice 1
Hymn   "Come, All Christians, Be Committed"
John 13:1; Matt. 26:26-28   Voice 2
Communion Hymn   "Beneath the Cross of Jesus"
         COMMUNION TIME, if appropriate

John 13:3-7, 12-17   Voice 3
Report of Servanthood (a review of last year's
    work)   Voice 4
Gift of Words (recognition of a special
    servant)   Voice 5
Hymn   "Reach Out and Touch"
Message (see below)
Commissioning of Officers (see below)
"So Send I You"   Trio Or Solo
Closing Prayer   An Elder
Hymn, verse 1   "All for Jesus"

MESSAGE: THE SERVANT'S SERVANT
JOHN 13:4, 12-17
by Mary Ellen Lantzer

To choose to be a servant is unusual. Why would one ever choose the exhaustion and frustration that goes with the job of being a servant — especially when one could choose instead to be the master, the one in charge? Who would choose the weary shoes of a servant? — All of us who have chosen to follow the Master-Servant.

It's a very serious business to follow a Master such as we have. For Christ calls us to be servants, not lords. What's more, we are called to be servant of *other* servants! Now, it seems reasonable to serve God — after all, He is powerful. He created us. He brought us into eternal life. We want to show our gratitude for all that the Lord has done. But sometimes it seems a bit too much to be asked to serve other *servants*.

For one thing, it's not very — well, it's not very impressive, for one thing. To serve other servants means we are often called to serve those already weary from their own work. There won't be many side benefits. And we all know how little praise or gratitude will ever reach our ears. Being a servant's servant is — well, to be honest, being a servant's servant isn't very self-fulfilling.

If we are weighing the benefits of being a servant, there isn't much to recommend it. I guess that is why Jesus had to try one last time to get his disciples to understand that they were being called into *servanthood*. Not for glory. Nor money. Nor personal satisfaction. But service on behalf of others.

97

So, just who *IS* this Lord who calls us to serve?
(Read John 13:4-7, 12-17)

That night which Jesus spent with the disciples would be his leavetaking. In a short time the meal would be over and the shadow of a cross would darken their lives. If there was any unfinished work — any unfinished lesson — it had to be done *now*.

SO — Jesus rises from the table and moves across the room on feet still dusty and road-weary from the roads of Galilee and Judea. There is a towel. And a wash basin, it's water still fresh and unused. Not one of the disciples thought it HIS responsibility to be at the door, washing the feet of the others as they arrived. That's a *servant's* job, not a disciple's.

Jesus brings the basin over and cleans the dirt off their feet, wiping them with a towel. Peter, who, along with John, was in charge of the meal arrangements, realizes that he has overlooked this detail and is embarrassed. He tries to decline Jesus' help, but Jesus insists on cleaning his feet, too. The lesson is too important to be passed over lightly.

Twelve pairs of feet later, Jesus straightens up and takes his seat at the table, looking around at his beloved friends. This time, they *must* understand. If not, three years of watching Him and living with Him would be wasted, for the kingdom He meant to leave behind could never survive arrogance or ambition.

"Can you understand what this means?" He asks. "If I am your *Teacher*, then learn to do this same thing. If I *am* your Lord, then practice my way of life. I have modeled this kind of service so you can see what I want you to do. If you think you are above serving this way, then you are no servants of mine; for I am not above doing it. *It is not enough just to think or talk of being a servant — you must actually get down and SERVE.*

If we don't want to be servants, then we have chosen the wrong master, for Jesus Christ indeed emptied Himself and took on the form of a servant — for you and me. He calls us to follow Him into servanthood.

But how can we serve? What will it mean to follow this Master-Servant?

Perhaps it will bring the risk of being looked down on, as with the young girl Mary, who was willing to be the maidservant of God even if she were to be a public outcast. Mary, a deep-spirited young woman who pondered things in her heart, composed a beautiful hymn of praise to the God who uses servants. Luke includes it in his gospel account.

Or maybe you will serve like Anna, an 84-year-old widow who spent her days and nights in prayer and fasting. After seeing the Christ, she spoke of Him to all who had been waiting for word of God's redemption.

We don't even have to be in perfect health. Peter's mother-in-law had been sick in bed with a fever. Jesus touched her hand, the fever left her, and she immediately got up and served Him and the disciples.

And it was a sinful woman who came to Jesus' feet to worship and be forgiven, washing His feet with her tears and rubbing them with ointment that she brought in an alabaster jar.

Will you serve with your money, whether you are on aid or well-off? A poor, widowed woman did not let her poverty keep her from giving financially — even though her offering was only two of the tiniest coins: she still gave. Other women who had more resources – like Mary Magdalene, Joanna (whose husband worked for Herod), Susanna, and others – traveled with Jesus and the disciples, providing for them out of their means.

Can we be ready to serve like Mary and Martha, sisters who were close friends of the Lord? Mary sat at His feet as a student. In the last days of Jesus' life Mary, helpless to stop His death, shared a deeply moving ritual which anointed Christ for burial. Martha often prepared meals for the Lord, but also had enough time to learn: her faith in Jesus held firm even in the midst of bereavement.

A woman in Samaria left her water at the well in order to return to the town and tell people of the Living Water – the One for whom they had been waiting.

Some women at the cross found all they could give was their presence as a beloved friend died a terrible death. Later, they checked to see what needed to be done to complete the burial arrangements and returned as soon as they could with the necessary materials.

Mary Magdalene and the other Mary were commissioned to carry news of the resurrection of Jesus back to the grieving disciples. They continued to tell of the good news, even when no one would believe their word.

Making clothes and doing other acts of love have long been done as beautiful service. Dorcus was well-known for her ministry with a needle. Yet Lydia found her service in hospitality for church workers and in sharing with other women in a prayer group. Priscilla's servanthood required that she risk her own life to help a missionary in danger. She was known for her teaching and was involved in the work of the church in several cities. And we must not forget to imitate Lois and Eunice, who made sure that young Timothy learned the Scripture and supported his decision to go into missionary work.

How do we serve? In all these ways — no matter what public opinion will be, or how old we are, or what our health is, or whether we have failed in the past. We serve by giving sacrificially out of our poverty — and if we have been blessed with abundant resources, we may be able to work along side of and support those in ministry.

Your service may be studying, teaching, making things for others, or leading in prayer groups. Perhaps it will be raising children to know God and His word, then helping them find ways to serve. It can be helping grieving families or being with someone during the last hours of life. Your call may even be spreading the news of the resurrected Christ even when no one listens — even at the risk of your own life. *And sometimes it is also the simple task of washing the grimy dust off feet worn out from following Jesus.* We are asked to be servants. We have much work to do.

You see, *listening* isn't enough. The disciples had been listening to Jesus for months. Hearing meant nothing without action. The blessing of being a servant of the Lord only comes to those who hear the word of the Master and obey it. Put it into practice. Do the will of the Lord.

101

Hearing Jesus' request and not acting is foolish. After all, we do claim that He is our Lord. Hearing our Lord but not responding is about as foolish as putting up a house on a foundation of sand. No one with any sense would do that. Everyone knows that a house is put on a solid foundation. And everyone knows that a servant does the will of the master — or really cannot be called a servant.

We serve a Lord who has asked us to serve others. Our service may not be very glamorous. It will involve a lot of hard work. And we probably will hear very little praise. But remember — it is our Lord's will. We are called to serve.

Statement of Charge

The women who stand before you are those who have been prayerfully chosen to be your special servants for the coming year. The work we do as women in the fellowship of the whole church is immeasurable, and these officers will be largely responsible for its success. We charge you in the presence of the Lord in His house to be worthy women in your lives and influence and to fulfill your responsibilities as unto Him. If you so promise, will you say "we do." Because no leaders can be effective without wholehearted support, we ask all who will give them the needed support to say "we do."

Will last year's officers please come forward and present the emblems of servant leadership to their new counterparts. As you can see these emblems are the towels which have the Scripture reference of John

13:14. Keep them to remind you of the privilege you have of following the Lord's example. (This may be followed by naming each officer of the previous year one by one and having each to present the towel to her counterpart for the coming year.)

An Evening of Remembrance
An Installation Service

The purpose of this program is two-fold: first, to remember the women who have served the church in the past in an outstanding manner but are now deceased and comprise much of the spiritual heritage of the church; and secondly to install the new officers the group, inspiring them to see themselves as becoming part of the same history.

This would be an ideal time for the women to be in charge of the evening service. In that case, the communion service would be an essential part of such remembrance. Arrangements should be made far in advance with the elders of the congregation.

Program Preparation: In some churches there may be only one or two women to be remembered; with others there may be several. As preparation, research the church's records and/or interview some members of the family or close friends so that these spiritual biographies can be as complete as possible. Items of interest, such as photographs, old bulletins, paper clippings, and other memorabilia should be collected

103

for display in a "Hall of Fame." Be sure to give a special invitation to family members or special friends who have aided in the research for the service.

During the program a time should be set aside to honor these women "who being dead yet speak." The persons who did the interviewing for these women would be the logical individuals to do this, but it would not be necessary.

Room Preparation: If this service is to be the evening worship, the regular sanctuary would be used. Unless there are objections to having objects other than the emblems on the communion table, a length of chain symbolizing the bonds of servanthood may be placed upon it. Otherwise, the chain may be arranged on the small table or podium from which the installation officer will speak. Chain in various weights and metals may be found in the hardware section of many stores. The original length of chain can be cut at the store into a number of pieces consistent with the number of officers to be installed. These smaller lengths will then be tied back together with velvet ribbon or cord. Each officer will receive a length of chain with ribbon during the installation. Brass-colored chain with crimson ribbon or silver colored chain with royal purple will be effective.

Concluding the service, the group could be invited to visit the "Hall of Fame" and fellowship with one another. The display should be in the same room as the dessert table. Finger foods should be provided and chairs arranged in groups for conversations or sharing of memories.

Program Presentation

Instrumental Music Medley
This should be a medley of old favorites of the past, songs perhaps not in the current song books but known and loved by the "long timers" of the congregation.

Praise Through Remembrance
The song leader chooses three or four songs which the congregation should be able to sing from memory — first stanza only.

God's "Hall of Fame"

Hebrews 11:1-12	Speaker 1
Hebrews 11:17-38	Speaker 2

Congregational Response: Hebrews 12:1
"Therefore, since we are surrounded by so great a cloud of witnesses, let us also lay aside every weight, and sin which clings so closely, and let us run with perseverance the race that is set before us, looking to Jesus the pioneer and perfecter of our faith who for the joy that was set before Him endured the cross, despising the shame, and is seated at the right hand of the throne of God.

Communion: In Remembrance of Him

Spiritual Biographies: These are like Abel — though they are dead, yet they speak to us.

Installation of Officers: (See Below)

Prayer: Minister

105

Installation Service

Installing Officer: Will the officers of the past year come forward and stand on my left. We have heard again from the women who have served us in years gone by, and we recognize that you have added to that history by your service in the past year to this congregation by presiding as the officers and as such, ministered to the women of this congregation. We wish to thank you for the time spent in this ministry and ask God's blessing on you in the coming year as you continue to serve Him who ever lives to serve us.

And now will the new officers please come forward and stand on my right.

We want to welcome you to a special fellowship — not a fellowship of honor, but a fellowship of real service. Remembering our Lord Jesus in His ministry, we know it will not be an easy road, but it is one in which you may truly be Servants. Those who have gone before you have found it to have enriched their lives. May you begin this year with God's blessing and with our full support and willingness to help.

On the table before me, there lies a length of chain tied with scarlet ribbon. The chain has long been a symbol of servanthood; and as servants of Christ we find it fitting reminder of our relationship with Him. The chain, however, reminds us also of the importance of unity and continuity. The chain you see is formed into one by ties representing loyalty not only to one another, but to those who preceded us.

Will you, *(name outgoing president,)* please untie the first segment of the chain representing the presi-

106

dency and give it your counterpart, *(name incoming president)*. (All other officers may be presented in the same way.)

It is our hope that each of you will find a significant place in your home to hang your chain to remind you of those who have gone before you and of your place in the spiritual heritage of the church.

Will the congregation please stand as our minister leads us in closing prayer. After the prayer we will adjourn to the "Hall of Fame.

Treasures in Earthen Vessels

❖

"We have this treasure in earthen vessels, that the excellency of the power may be of God, and not of us." II Cor. 4:7 KJV

An Installation Service

Although this service may be adapted to be used alone, the authors suggest that it be the main thrust of a council meeting (luncheon or dinner).

Table decorations: In keeping with the these, tables may be decorated with shards of broken clay pots in which tiny dried flowers have been hot glued. These can be coordinated with your napkins, keeping in mind that since clay is not very colorful you should keep to rich earth tones if possible. In the center of each table place a plant in a clay pot. Please note: these decoration will be used in the installation service later.

Serving Suggestions: This can truly be a "pot" luck meal. Request that the members bring a dish in a pot. New clay pots lined with foil can be used to bake chicken pot pies or casseroles. They may also hold gelatin salads or raw vegetable "bouquets." Rolls, cookies and many desserts can be served in this way. Have fun!

Note: If you are invited to be the installing officer at another church, perhaps you could share these plans with the group who is inviting you. Usually suggestions are welcome.

All business and the outgoing president's message should precede the installation service.

Installation Service

Song: "Have Thine Own Way"

Installing Officer: So common was the making of pottery to Jewish life that the prophet Jeremiah likened the destruction of Israel by pagan Babylonia to earthen vessels dashed into shards because of their idolatry. A nation selected by God as "Chosen vessels," was to become as a trash heap — utterly useless to God and to themselves!

What contributes to brokenness in our day? Ask any group and it will give answers such as these: lack of unified purpose, complacency or indifference, procrastination, pride, (who gets the credit?), pessimism (it won't work here), lack of persistence, little vision or insight, no accountability, poor communication.

We've all heard these reasons and have probably been guilty of assigning these frailties to others. But we are all broken shards without each other.

The apostle Paul pointed out in Romans that God as Potter has appointed each of us to service and is very blunt in pointing out that we all must do our share as God has gifted us. Let us listen to a favorite scripture, Romans 12, to remind ourselves of the positive virtues of working together.

Selected Reader: reads Romans 12: 3-14

Installing Officer: Will all the officers to be installed please come forward, when your name is called, bringing with you a broken shard from the table.

As you can see from the table decorations, a small shard standing alone can perhaps lend beauty to a small space, but how much more effective is the unbroken pot you see in the center of your tables.

_____, our outgoing president, will recognize our new president by bringing her a token of unity, a potted plant, from the center of a table and in turn accept from her the shard, the symbol of brokenness. This will be a reminder of cooperation needed for the new president's success.

(The other officers may be recognized in the same way, naming the outgoing officer as she comes forward.)

Installing Officer (addresses the whole group): Will you accept these women as your leaders for the coming year and will you support them in a unity of spirit and readiness to assist them that will make of this year's work a beautiful thing in God's eyes? If so, will you say, "We will."

Response: We will.

Installing Officer: (addresses new officers): Will you new officers pledge yourselves to minister to the women in this church and to lead them responsibly in the work that is to be done? If so, respond, "We will.

Officers Respond: We will.

New President: Short personal response, if desired, followed by the closing prayer:

Father of unity in whom is no brokenness, be with us in this year of work and help us keep our eyes on those things which are really important in Your eyes. Help us not to "think more highly of ourselves than we ought to think." We realize that not many of us are alabaster boxes filled with fragrant nard, but we all are useful vessels. We want to be used. Make us truly able. In Jesus' name. Amen

Let Us Pray
An Installation Service

———❖———

The following installation service, composed of prayers in one form or another, may seem strange at first but if you decide to introduce your officers through prayer, be prepared for changed lives. This service would be particularly fitting to open a year committed to development of a significant prayer life individually and as a people.

Room Preparation: If your group is small enough (20-30), form a tight circle of chairs. You will want to sit for at least part of your prayer time for it will be extended. If your group is large, form several circles, preferably not more than the number of officers to be installed so that one new officer and her outgoing counterpart can sit in each circle. You will need no decorations for this service and they are actually discouraged. NOTE: A meal and business meeting can be held before the installation or refreshments and a time of visitation can be held after the installation but another room should be used for this.

Leader Preparation: One person may be chosen to conduct the meeting or the responsibility may be divided among several people. The leader(s), one(s) known for an active prayer life, should spend several large blocks of time in prayer in the weeks before the installation. In addition to prayer, the leader may want to read some books on prayer.

A Word of Explanation: The prayers provided are samples. They may be used as they are, expanded, or replaced with the leader's own words. It would be well to follow the topics as a guideline if personal prayers are offered.

Installation Service of Prayer

Introduction: Explain to the group that the entire evening will be given to prayer as you introduce and install your new officers. Plan to vary positions (standing, sitting and even kneeling) so that members will not become uncomfortable. Many people like to hold hands during prayer time but this is a very uncomfortable position for extended prayer. Members may want to touch each other as a means of expressing unity but a hand on another's arm or a momentary squeeze of the hand may be less distracting than ongoing hand holding.

Note: Different women can pray for each officer. If you prefer, you can print the entire program and have the starred sections read in unison by all of the women. Other hymns that could be used during the service are "Be Thou My Vision," "'Tis the Blessed Hour of Prayer," and "More Holiness Give Me."

Opening Prayer: Singing of "Let's Just Praise the Lord" or "Take Time to be Holy."

Prayer for President: God of leadership, Sovereign of the universe, we come this day to ask your blessing upon our new president, _____. In our world, Lord, we tend to think of leadership roles as roles of power and honor. Men and women strive to achieve these positions in order to gain control over others. But, Lord, we come to ask Your blessings on _____ in her role as servant leader, in imitation of Jesus Christ. She has agreed to work with and for us to Your glory, to seek no personal honor, but to be in this office at this time as her gift to us and therefore to You. We know that _____ has many gifts *(name specific gifts)* – and we ask you to bless these gifts and increase them for the benefit of all.

Give her good health, a strong voice and strength of spirit so that she may execute her duties without undue stress. Give her wisdom to recognize our needs, fill her with ideas for execution and surround her with Your Spirit in her waking and sleeping hours so that all we do in the coming year is under Your

112

control.

Lord, we ask that you bless her with our support. Give us willing hearts and ready hands so that we may follow through and uphold the plans that our president makes with and for us. Let us give honor to her who seeks no honor, appreciation to the one who serves us, and let Your love flow from us to her and back again so that the world will see how we love one another.

Oh, all wise Leader, we bring before you at this time our friend and leader, _____. Wrap her in Your love and fill her with your goodness that she may be a worthy servant in the coming year. In the name of the servant of all, Jesus Christ, Amen.

Instrumental Interlude of quiet prayerful music.

Prayer for the Vice-President: Oh, One God, who asks to be first in our lives, we bring before you now the person and life of _____. We have chosen her for second place, to be Vice-President of our group this year. Our society makes jokes about vice-presidents, Lord. We talk as if they were useless appendages to the office of president. We tend to hope the president won't get sick or die so that we will have to deal with the vice-president, the one to whom we have given the booby prize of a useless office. But Lord, we have not chosen our Vice-President lightly. We recognize her value as a strong and sure sounding board for our president. We acknowledge her own personal strengths and gifts, *(name strengths)*, and we recognize her as co-worker, not as second string.

We ask that you bless her with the ability to give

wise advice and counsel to the president and to move among the membership in such a way as to inspire us to love and good works. Give her also a strong body and a peaceful life so that she can concentrate on the task set before her. Let her life among us be an example of purity, lovingkindness, and joy in Your service.

We ask for ourselves the willingness to encourage her and to reward her efforts with cooperation. Allow the Spirit to flow between us so that there is a wonderful excitement in our journey together this year.

We present for your everlasting love, _____ . Bless her family, her work, and her relationships within the church and accept her as Your servant and ours for the coming year. In the name of Him who humbled Himself to become like us, Amen.

Musical Interlude for personal reflection and prayer.

Prayer for the Secretary: Lord God of stories, who saw fit to record for us the history of Your people, we ask you now to bless _____ , our Secretary. It is she who will record our story in the coming year, who will take note of our deeds, our plans, and our activities throughout the year. Minutes are often regarded as boring, Lord, something we have to endure at meetings so we can get on with the important stuff, but minutes are important because they record the history of people. They are where we can turn to assess our direction, to determine if we have kept on course and followed through with our commitments. They, and the one who records them, are important in the life of our group. Along with the minutes, there are the letters, Lord — the little thank-you notes that brighten people's days and encourage them to keep serving and the letters of inquiry and statements of intent that must be written so that the flow of service can continue smoothly.

So, Master Record Keeper, bless our secretary, with a keen mind, a ready pen, and a good command of the language so that her words will be accurate and full of understanding. Keep her body whole and her heart from worry so that she may be an instrument of communication among us, our missionaries, our speakers, and all who need from us the written word.

And, Lord, we apologize for being impatient people, who often would prefer not to hear what we did at our last meeting. Teach us the importance of good record keeping and help us listen with discerning minds, making corrections as needed and affirming the truth of what we will accomplish in the months ahead. Give us appreciation for the time needed to accurately convey the message of commitment we feel through the reports of our votes, decisions and deeds.

In the name of Jesus Christ, the Word made flesh among us, we present our friend, _____, for Your blessing, Amen.

Musical Interlude (piano, flute, violin or other instrument).

Prayer for the Treasurer: O, Giver of All Gifts, Owner of All Treasure, we come now to beseech a gift of blessing upon our new Treasurer, _____. Into her hands we will entrust our monetary contributions to the work of this group. She will have the special task of helping us develop a budget so give her a generous heart to discern needs so that she can encourage our generosity. It is her skills of *(list skills)* that have determined our selection of her as our treasurer. Strengthen those skills so that she can keep accurate accounts and prepare timely reports of our money collected and disbursed.

Bless this, our keeper of the funds, with financial security in her own life so that she not be burdened with problems of money while she attends to the money we will offer to your service. Keep her mind keen and her memory sharp so that she can tend to the tedious work of bookkeeping with joy.

And Wonderful Giver, open our hands to the needy and our pocketbooks to those dying in sin, so that our group's checkbook may reflect the priorities of tenderness and concern. Instill in us a willingness to become involved in the financial affairs of this body so that we become co-workers with our treasurer. Let us ask questions which demonstrate a real interest, and require of ourselves and our treasurer an accountability in your eyes.

In appreciation for the greatest Gift, Jesus Christ, we pray, Amen.

Responsive Prayer:

New Officers:	Creator God , we praise your wonderous works.
All Women:	We praise your holy name.
Officers:	Lord, we accept your guidance.
Women:	And we also.
Officers:	Grant us vision and wisdom for leadership.

Women: Grant us the humility to follow.

Officers: Fill us with your Spirit and grant us grace.

All: For thine is the kingdom and the power and the glory forever. Amen.

Closing Prayer Song: "O, Master, Let Me Walk With Thee" or "Take My Life, and Let It Be"

The
Soup Pot

❖

An Accumulation of Seed Ideas

Chapter 5

"If I could just come up with an idea, I could go on from there, but my well is dry!" If you have ever been in a quandary (and what leader hasn't!), you may find something in the Soup Pot which will get you started. Sometimes getting the first serving out of a catsup bottle is the hardest. Soloman said there is nothing new under the sun, and but we hope you may find an idea new to you or be reminded of one you had forgotten.

Getting Acquainted

"I was a stranger and you took me in"
(Matthew 25:35c, NIV)

THE CHURCH THAT TAKES THE CAKE

How quickly do you respond to new visitors to your church? Be known as "the church that takes the cake" by enlisting your best cooks to volunteer a freshly baked cake to be delivered in greeting by another volunteer on Sunday afternoon to that morning's visitors. Often this will result in an invitation to come in and visit. Programs of the church which might be of interest to the visitor can be explained. A fresh loaf of homemade bread is also a delicious way to welcome a family during the week following their visit to the church.

PARTY FOR NEW MEMBERS

Help new members in your congregation become better acquainted with you and you with them by inviting a group to a paper bag party. Each guest is asked to bring a sack with items which will be representative of the things important in his/her life. These can be such items as a golf ball, a sheet of music, a recipe book, or running shoe. This adult "show and tell" will be fun for everyone. You will learn things about each other you would never have known otherwise.

MYSTERY MEMBER

How well do you know the home folks? Mystery Member will expand your knowledge of each other while providing many a laugh. Try this getting-better-acquainted exercise in a large Bible School Class, a Women's Council meeting, or at Wednesday night fellowship dinners. The person in charge asks a member of the group to provide a list of ten clues to his/her identity that are little known by the group. The clues should be as neutral as possible and may be worded so as to be misleading as long as they are truthful. The person in charge then arranges the clues in order of difficulty (least known first) so as to keep the mystery as long as possible.

The clues are read one at a time in the meeting and members must stand to make a guess. When the mystery is solved, the mysterious member is asked to stand and any remaining clues are read. The one who has made the correct identification may be presented with a token gift or a white elephant. If the mystery is not solved, the mystery member gets the prize. This is a good way to start a class, but it should not be allowed to take up much class time. Make a point to continue this practice until all the people in the class have been featured as the Mystery Member, paying early attention to those who are little known or often ignored.

Ministering to One Another

"Each of you should look not only to your own interests, but also to the interests of others" (Philippians 2:4, NIV)

THINKING OF YOU

Plan to meet for breakfast in a local restaurant. Each person should bring one or more "thinking of you" type cards. The leader should come prepared with names and addresses of shut-ins, ill persons, or people who need encouragement. Even better, each person could come with a list, including persons who perhaps are not the church fellowship. Everyone should sign all cards and include a brief message if desired. Stamps and decorative seals should be provided. After this activity, give the cards to one person to mail.

BIRTHDAY CELEBRATION FOR ELDERLY SAINTS

Nearly every church is blessed with an older saint who continues to be a Christian example even though he/she is not physically able to work for Christ as he/she did in the past. These people should be remembered. Try one of the two following ways to make their birthdays special.

1) Have a special birthday party at the church or someone's home if the honored guest is able to attend. Suggest in the invitation that donations be made to a charity dear to the honoree's heart. Token gifts may also be brought to the party and cards are strongly encouraged. Have a notebook with plastic page covers on hand and insert the cards for safe keeping. Take plenty of pictures, including videos if possible.

2) If the honoree is shut-in, take a small group to the home, including some children. Calling beforehand to set the date is important. Since many older people have few real needs, the fun comes by providing a gift for every year of their lives. Attach a message to the outside of each package, wrapping like things together.

Use your imagination — a trip to the grocery and variety store will provide many cute ideas. Some examples with messages follow:

1 Birthday cake	Happy Birthday, Kathie Smith (always use personal names).
6 helium balloons	May these give you a lift.

12	aspirins (a small tin)	A little something for your aches.
1	naked baby doll	To remind you of your humble beginnings.
12	bendable straws	To help you get the most out of life.
8	postage stamps	Keep in touch.
6	apples	A prescription for good health.
2	pretty wash cloths	You'll clean up with these.
6	light bulbs	Here's to brighter days ahead.
4	rolls bathroom tissue	Something no one can do without.
4	tea bags	Polly put the kettle on.
3	cans of Pepsi	Come join the NOW generation.
1	can of soup	Simply super supper.
5	purse-size packs of tissue	For those wonderfully sad or happy times — like today.
2	warm socks (1 pair)	Something for iron-poor blood.
7	names and phone numbers written in large print	A very present help in a time of need.
3	safety pins	We want to help hold you together.
1	nice gift	Chosen especially for your friend with your own message.

Note: This idea can be used for people of any age. A Chinese student who celebrated a 27th birthday shortly after coming to America was treated to a party where all guests were to bring 27 of anything. Gifts such as flowers, toothpicks, safety pins, matches, paper clips, index cards, Cokes, vegetables and dollars were presented.

A SECRET PAL WITH A PURPOSE

Feel separated from the young people of your congregation? Do you have a desire to make contact, provide encouragement but don't really know how and are afraid they won't listen? Try an adult-youth secret pal arrangement. To work, this secret pal service must be kept a deep dark secret. No one outside the circle of those who are the Secret Pals is to know about it until the end of the year.

1. Select a number of the youth equal to the women (or men) who want to be encouragers.

2. Assign each encourager a young person for a secret pal.

3. Encouragers write notes to pals to tell them they will be hearing from them for the next year.

4. Each month a note, or gift, or both is sent to the young person. Gifts should not be expensive but thoughtfully selected. Bookmarks, fast food coupons, one or two dollars, books, inexpensive jewelry, a cherished item of the encourager's along with an accompanying story about the item all make good gifts. The main thing is to provide encouraging words. Gifts and notes can be left in mailboxes, on door

steps, and sent through the mail. Christmas, birthdays and other holidays as well as honors the student has received should be acknowledged.

5. At the end of the year, all the young people and their parents are invited to a party where the encouraging adults are revealed to the young recipients. Take two pictures of each encourager-youth team and give one to each member. A pair of kissing angels makes a nice final gift to give to each young person at the party. You may never know the long term results of this secret pal experience, but in the short term all will have an interesting and rewarding year.

Reusing Our Resources
❖

"And the Lord God took the man and put him in the Garden of Eden to work it and take care of it" (Genesis 2:15, NIV).

DOUBLE DUTY FLOWERS

1. When planning to use flowers to decorate tables at a church banquet, plan ahead a list of shut-ins to whom the flowers will be taken afterward. The flowers should be accompanied by a personal note including perhaps a reference to occasions when this person has been among you regularly. Include also a copy of the program for the evening with a recognization of the shut-ins printed in the program. The note and spe-

cial mention will make the flowers special and not just leftovers from a party.

2. Make someone's day by presenting him/her with your centerpieces. Determine those in your community who might never have received flowers of their own and plan to deliver the flowers to them with an expression of your love. Suggested persons are foster children or children in children's homes, residents of group homes for the mentally retarded or mentally ill, and church members without families. Don't overlook men and boys in this activity. Be sure the flowers are specifically for one person, not for the group. This individual attention can be a springboard to a relationship with the one honored.

3. Potted flower centerpieces may also be donated to the church for planting. In this case, it would be necessary to consult the person or committee which has charge of the lawn and grounds of the church.

RECYCLING PARTY

Christian people who take their stewardship of the earth (Gen. 1:28) seriously should be those who support, or even initiate their community's plans for recycling as one way to be responsible for the earth's care. Plan a program in which you can reach your church family and enlist their involvement. Have initially a "Recycling Party" and ask each person who attends to bring an example of recycling already done in their own homes. It will be surprising how many different things we already do and are even unaware of. This activity could be held in connection with Earth Day. Be sure this party results in an ongoing project.

Just For Fun

❖

"A merry heart does good like a medicine: but a broken spirit drieth the bones" (Proverbs 17:22, KJV).

PIG IN A POKE

What is a poke? A bag for carrying things. A "pig in a poke" is anything bought or acquired without first examining it. This party can be a variation of the white elephant party. It can be strictly for fun as exchanges or Chinese auctions, or it can have a specific purpose, such as a shower for a family who has lost belongings in a fire or flood. Each person who attends is to bring an item in a "poke," and everything from prizes you might want to award to the food served should be in a "poke." Table decorations can be "picnic casual," using checked cloths, country lanterns, and PIGS. If you know a good storyteller, there are several delightful stories and rhymes about pigs available. Use your imagination — you will have a party to oink about!

INSTANT ENTERTAINING

Encourage your members to be more hospitable by providing an evening "a la cooking school" for your Women's Council meeting. Enlist the aid of several tal-

129

ented hostesses who can provide demonstrations of simple-to-make dishes and tips for creating a party atmosphere with little work. Arrange for three or four cooking centers and plan to prepare several easy and quick recipes to be served immediately. These can be salads, desserts or main dishes depending on your situation. Provide copies of the recipes and the tips for entertaining on budgeted time and money.

The Poor Among You

"She opens her arms to the poor and extends her hands to the needy" (Proverbs 31: 20,NIV).

A DIFFERENT KIND OF POTLUCK

Church potluck dinners are often made-up of expensive casseroles rich in nuts, broccoli, and creams. In a world of hunger, our self-indulgence seems sinful at times. In order to make us aware of the limited budgets many people survive on, introduce your group to a different kind of potluck supper. Instruct everyone to bring a dish that will serve ten people and costs no more than $2.50. The cost of seasoning (butter, vanilla, and so forth) must be considered. Creative cooking results, so that good, simple food you haven't had in years may turn up on the table. A collection of food or money can be taken at the end of the meal to donate to the hungry of your community or the world.

A REAL THANKSGIVING

One church family recently observed Thanksgiving in this way. When the dinner had been cooked and all were seated in eager anticipation of the feast, the mother served the father only and joined the rest of the family while they watched him eat. Surprise was followed by moanings and groanings and protests of "That's not fair!" All ate more gratefully when they were served only after being reminded that many of the peoples of the world view America as they were viewing the father eating bountifully while much of the world starves. Why not try this at your house — today.

Another family gave thanks for the dirty dishes, which gave mute testimony to an abundant meal.

A LIVING LOVE FUND

How does your church family handle financial crises among its members? Does it ignore them or have a poorly funded, inactive benevolent committee? Then perhaps you should begin a Living Love Fund to meet needs as they arise. The fund should be separate from the general fund of the church and used primarily to help members of the congregation and only occasionally for unusual needs outside the fellowship. The distribution of funds should be held in confidence by a committee of three members who make all decisions concerning distribution. The committee should be appointed for limited terms on a rotating basis.

Persons in need, their friends, and/or the ministerial staff may approach the committee with requests. The committee should also be alert to needs and offer help to anyone who is out of work for an extended period of time or has unusual expenses beyond his/her control. This fund can provide a valuable means of expressing concern and teaching people both to give and receive as life situations change.

The fund can be started by seed money from the Women's Council and Sunday School Classes, and maintained by continuing gifts from these groups but primarily by love offerings, memorials and honorariums from individuals. The congregation should be reminded often of the fund and kept informed of current balances and distributions while keeping the recipients' names confidential.

Fund Raising

❖

"We will not neglect the house of our God" (Nehemiah 10:39c, NIV).

ARMCHAIR BAKE SALE

Save the time and energy women have expended on bake sales which have little return! Invite women to bring the recipe and an offering amounting to the cost of baked goods they ordinarily would have made and come to a coffee hour. Coffee and homemade sweet rolls may be served. Women may share their recipes, relax and have fun while meeting their financial goals.

YARD SALE

Does your church need redoing? Does your nursery need a warm rug for little toddlers to sit on? Or does your sanctuary need a carpet? Why not have a "YARD SALE"? Estimate the yardage needed for your project, select the material, and encourage the membership to buy a yard. The sale could extend over a short period of time or it could be held at a stated time and location with a "yard sale" picnic, luncheon, or potluck dinner for the whole church.

Put It In Writing

❖

"The Lord moved the heart of Cyrus King of Persia to make a proclamation throughout his realm and to put it in writing" (Ezra 1:1, NIV).

A DEVOTIONAL BOOKLET

Give your congregation a gift for Christmas and Easter. Create a devotional booklet written by members of your own fellowship to be used by the families in the church. It's a rather simple venture, but time consuming and rewarding.

Start about three months before you want to hand out your booklets (September 1 for a December 1 distribution). You can do it in less time, but the quality is likely to be less or the editor exhausted. Decide on a format — will you have just the devotional or will you include a printed scripture, a scripture reading and prayer as many of the published devotional books do? Decide on a word limit. Three hundred words will do nicely for a half sheet of typing paper.

Ask known writers in your congregation to write one or more devotionals using the guidelines you provide. Also ask for volunteers from among the congregation. Be sure everyone knows that there will be editing needed. Don't ask for more material than you can use unless you are willing to have someone disappointed because his or her work was not published.

Have a group of editors who go over the material and put it in its final form for publishing. Be sure your layout is attactive and well typed. Using the church copier make a booklet for each church family plus a few extras for visitors. In December a booklet of red, green and white paper would be nice. For the Easter edition, you might want to use pastels or a gold and purple combination.

Distribute the booklets the Sunday before families are to begin using them. You may choose to have devotionals for the month of December and the month preceeding Easter or just for a week or two before the holiday. Whatever you decide, know that your congregation will profit from the experience of writing and reading together. You may find this devotional booklet a natural springboard to the more ambitious project of a regular careletter (a newsletter for women).

A WOMEN'S CARELETTER

Have you ever been asked several times for the recipe of a casserole or cake you took to the last church dinner? Have you ever missed a wedding and wanted to know what happened? Have you missed a program at church and longed for a blow-by-blow account? Have you wished you knew more about the new woman who just placed membership with your congregation? Have you heard of a shut-in and wondered why she was so important to the older members of the church? Have you wished you knew what happened to a child who had been in your Sunday Bible Study? Do you wish you had a way to share the spiritual experiences of some of the church's quiet people? Do you like to read and often wish for recommendations of good books?

If you can answer "yes" to any of the above questions, your women's group would profit from its own newsletter. While the women's newsletter is similiar to a church newsletter, it has an entirely different purpose and flavor.

Women's newsletters are designed to bring women closer together through sharing of themselves. As such, they might well be called careletters rather than newsletters. They are basically designed to tell what happened and not just what's going to happen. If you would like to start a careletter, here are some suggestions.

Put out a call for women who would be interested in working on the careletter and meet with them. Brainstorm about such things as content, assignments, name, frequency of publication, and means of distribution. Select an editor with writing skills who is willing to coordinate your publication. Once different columns or departments for the careletter are established, assistant editors can be selected. Example: A Food Editor if you are going to have recipes, a Book Editor if you are going to have book reports.

Determine how you will pay for the publication and distribution. Most churches now have copiers which make publication much less expensive than in the past. If you mail your newsletter, the church may be willing to absorb the cost. Remember you must mail at least two hundred copies to get low mailing rates. Take care to observe postal rules from the beginning so that your operation will work smoothly.

Once you have the groundwork laid, the fun of writing begins. Be sure your paper carries articles of interest to a wide variety of women. Not everybody likes recipes, but many people do. One or two an issue will be enough. Be sure to include one or two inspirational articles per careletter. An occasional poem written by a member, a short sketch of a newcomer or a long-timer, circle news and activites all make good reading. Favorite Bible verses of the women, and reasons why they are favorites, can be a regular column. Don't forget the news — good news primarily — births, marriages, trips, prizes, honors, but also the illnesses and deaths. Steer clear of gossip and private pains. It's not a no-no to mention a man in the careletter but he perhaps could be identified as Mary Smith's husband, John — quite a switch from "John Smith's wife, Mary."

No matter how well written a publication is, it won't be well received unless it is attractively presented. Use plenty of white space, a reasonably large type and avoid crowding the articles. Add interest with sketches. Avoid using photographs unless you can get a good reproduction. There are picture copying grids available to use with photographs being reproduced on copiers that greatly improve results. One such grid, called Copyscreen-2, is put out by Graphic Products Corporation.

Be sure to date your publications and perhaps use volume and number as well. Copies should be kept for the church archives. If your fellowship is a part of the restoration movement (Disciples of Christ, Independent Christian, or Churches of Christ), consider sending copies to the Disciples of Christ Historical Society, Nashville. Tennessee. Copies should be kept through the year and mailed to the Society yearly. The Society has received a few women's records in the past but is most willing to include women's work in the archives of our movement.

APPENDIX

Number 1
Sample Letter for Use by New President

Date:

Dear Friend,

We are women, all of us. We are diverse: fat, thin, short, tall, some college grads and others not. We are skilled in professions, needlework, child care and many other things. We are single, married, widowed, and divorced. We are diverse, but we have one thing in common. All of us have our names on the membership roll of (_____Church). We attend regularly, occasionally or not at all. We are committed, slightly committed, ill and cannot come, angry and will not come, have moved away and go elsewhere, or discouraged and long to be inspired.

What can I say to all of you that will have meaning individually to such a wide variety of women? Space is limited. I must be concise. Three things must suffice.

1. YOU are important to me. If we are friends, I long for continued friendship. If we are strangers, I long to get acquainted. Friend or stranger, I long to know you better, and to have our strengths and our weaknesses intermingle for the building up of all. I want you to have a close relationship with at least two or three other women at (name of your congregation).

2. You have something to offer. Because of our diversity of gifts, skills, education, wisdom, and stage of life, we each have something unique to offer the body of Christ in the way of service. Perhaps you are already offering your gifts to Christ for His use in the body and the world. If so, I encourage you. Perhaps, however, you have never been encouraged or asked to use your skills. If so, I would like to help you find a place of service.

3. You have needs. The flow of life is such that each of us experience, wounds from time to time. Perhaps for you it is a physical illness, your own or the illness of one you love.

141

Others have children who have brought great anguish of heart to mothers. Still others experience loneliness and depression. The causes of our pains are many. Others cannot solve our problems or heal the hurts, but we can all profit from a caring touch and a listening ear.

Because you are important, have something to offer, and have needs, I would like you to do two things for me. I would like you to let me know what you are thinking. How can the women's program of the church be of help to you? (Enclose a questionnaire to prompt response to this Question.) I would also like you to pray for the work of the women of the church, and especially for your elected leaders this year.

I am excited about the coming year. Our study this year will be _____ . I know that involvement in the women's groups of the church is not for everyone, but that as the year passes, you will find yourself very involved in the body of Christ, and that like Him, you will seek and find a place of service in the world.

Number 2
Suggested Reminders for "A Taste of Childhood" for inclusion in written program

Do You remember? ? ? ? ?
   ...chunk bologna
   ...bread you had to slice
   ...milk warm from the cow or fresh from *glass* bottles
        delivered to your door
   ...your first McDonald's hamburger
   ...wartime Hershey bars
   ...standing in line to buy bubble gum
   ...drive-in restaurants with car hops
   ...when everyone ate Sunday dinner at home
   ...rationing coupons for sugar and coffee
   ...grandmother's chocolate pies
   ...green apples (stolen from the neighbors)
   ...when you were ashamed to take country ham biscuits
        in your school lunch
   ..."cranked" home-made ice cream
   ...chunk ice from the iceman

Have you tried? ? ? ?
   ...Poptarts
   ...chicken McNuggets
   ...frozen pizza
   ...Fruit Rollups
   ...frozen yogurt
   ...oat bran
   ...soft shell tacos
   ...Lunchables
   ...Lite everything
   ...microwave popcorn

(Add your own old-timey food and modern fare.)

143

Enlarge pattern so that it fits the size paper you wish to use. Regular typing paper makes a good size. If desired, draw a door with a child beside it on the pattern.

Type text on separate paper and glue in place on pattern. Be sure to glue so when folded the writing comes out in the right place.

If you will need extra pages, make two patterns and fold together after printing. Using copier, copy desired number of pages, cut, and fold.

Pattern for Program
"A Taste of Childhood"

Number 3
A Stitch in Time
Quilt Show Skit
By Gail Phillips

Persona: Grandmother, daughter, and grand-daughter

Scene: Attic, light through uncurtained window falls on an old trunk, other old rejects scattered about. The grandmother seated on a old ladder back chair is digging into the old trunk.

DAUGHTER: Mama! What are you doing up here?

GRANDDAUGHTER: Wow! This place is a mess!

(Soft violin music "Long, Long Ago . . . ")

GRANDMOTHER: You were asking whether I had any old quilts you could have. It just got me thinking . . .

DAUGHTER: Why, Mama, I don't want anything you need, I just asked because I thought . . . well you know . . . they 're so stylish now. All our friends have them and . . .

GRANDMOTHER: I know honey. But, what do I need with these. They've been packed away up here since my own mother died. Look at this!

(She holds up an old quilt obviously made from scraps of clothing and feed-sacks.)

GRANDDAUGHTER: Whew! (holds her nose) It smells musty!

GRANDMOTHER: Well, it has a right to, that was made when I was a child. Your great-grandmother, my mother, made these — lots of them — all by hand and sold them for $3 a quilt — that was the only cash money she had to live on.

GRANDDAUGHTER: Three Dollars a quilt! Oh — I spend more than that when I go for a pizza with my friends. How long did it take to make one of those things?

GRANDMOTHER: I don't know that she counted her time. It was a skill she could use and still take care of the young 'uns at home. Do you see those carders over there?

GRANDDAUGHTER: Huh?

GRANDMOTHER: Those boards with the spikes in them?
(Granddaughter hands them to her grandmother.) My mama carded the cotton for the battin' for the quilts she made. (Demonstrate) Then when she got it all pieced and put up on the quiltin' frame, sometimes her friends would come in for a spell and help her.

(Violin softly changes to "Seein' Nellie Home")

(Grandmother can pull out other quilts, bedspreads from the chest to show them — ad lib anything appropriate.)

DAUGHTER: I hardly remember Grandma but when I look at these quilts I feel like she left a great legacy to us. What a demonstration of love and commitment! Every stitch is a part of her love and every block holds some memory of a dress worn, a feed-sack saved. She didn't waste anything, did she?
GRANDDAUGHTER: (picks up a quilt to examine it) Personally, I perfer my electric blanket!
DAUGHTER: Honey — they didn't have electricity.

(Violin plays "Love's Old Sweet Song")

GRANDMOTHER: Look, here's mother's old Bible. It is plenty worn! She especially loved I Corinthians 13. (Insert granddaughter's name), Why don't you read it for us?
GRANDDAUGHTER: (Reads I Corinthians 13 from King James or other older version.)
GRANDMOTHER: Really, the only thing they had enough of was Love — didn't always say so in words like we do now — but they lived it out day by day, sacrificially, so that we would have it better than they did. I'm glad you want these quilts. I'm delighted that you value them. All of this work won't have been in vain if you two can just inherit, with these old quilts, some of the love and dedication that went into them.

146

Number 4
The Tangram

The tangram is an age old-puzzle/toy enjoyed by the Chinese. While it is primarily for children, it is challenging for adults as well. The puzzle is comprised of a square cut into five triangles, one square, and one rhomboid. The Chinese have used it as the basis for thousands of figures and designs.

The tangram can make an interesting cover menu/program booklet and also be used as a puzzle during table time. The puzzles should be pre-cut from construction paper of various colors. The puzzle pieces should be put in envelopes and one puzzle placed at each table setting. Since this puzzle is not a jig-saw, it should not be put back together. It should be arranged in a new design, such as a bird or flower. Each person should try to make a design different from her neighbor.

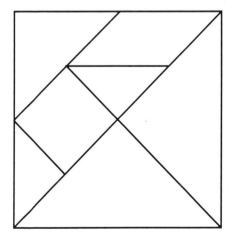

Number 5
Almond Tea
Oriental Festival

2 cups water boiled with
   1 and one half cup sugar and added to:
   2 tablespoons instant tea with lemon
   3 teaspoons vanilla
   3 teaspoons almond extract
   12 ounces frozen lemonade
2 quarts water added at serving time

This tea may be served in a punch bowl or heated and served as hot tea. This is excellent — inexpensive and different.